ANTHOLOGIA!

ISSUE 1

ANTHOLOGIA!

On a Time Between Stories

Daniella Libri Elias

Rose Mascaro

Kristina Garla

Courtney Zerafa

Beryl Crosher-Segers

Hannah Bishop

Stacey Howes

Kellie Hannah

Gina Kasmas

S. A. Sisika

Jessica Savage

First published in 2024 by The Kind Press

A catalogue record for this book is available from the National Library of Australia.

Cover design by Christa Moffitt, Christabella Designs
Text design by Nicola Matthews, Nikki Jane Design

Trade Paperback ISBN: 978-1-7635083-4-7
eBook ISBN: 978-0-6458993-6-8

We at The Kind Press acknowledge that Aboriginal and Torres Strait Islander peoples are the Traditional Custodians and the first storytellers of the lands on which we live and work; and we pay our respects to Elders past and present.

www.thekindpress.com

To the women—
may your stories shape us
across the lineage of time

CONTENTS

INTRODUCTION

The word 'Anthologia' traces its roots to the enchanting Greek language, embodying the phrase 'flower gathering.' Born from 'anthos' (flower) and 'legein' (to gather, to select), it emerged into English in the early 17th century, adorned with a metaphorical grace: a collection, meticulously chosen for its captivating beauty and profound significance.

Anthologia! celebrates this age-old tradition, unfolding a curated gathering of women storytellers in this powerful and inclusive Issue, *On a Time Between Stories* that are both universal and deeply personal. Written with verve and clear insights, the stories in this anthology, authored by eleven courageous women, emerge from the whispers of wisdom passed down through generations and deep connections of maternal lineage. They traverse the emotional landscapes of leaving homelands, the sensations of displacement, identity and belonging, and the enduring scars left by oppression. They sing an ode to women's rage and retell the myth of Athene and Medusa, reveal the protective fierceness of a mother's love, the resilience demonstrated by cancer survivors, and emotional safety and inclusion in women's lives.

These stories shine with essential truths about love, womanhood, and the timeless struggle to define ourselves and find love within our inner landscapes, embodying life's liminal moments. Together, these women write courageously, underscoring the vital role of documenting our stories to create a braver, more beautiful world.

Anthologia! is a call to all of us to adorn our own brief time with as much love, wisdom and, most importantly, beauty as possible. When women are the storytellers, we alter traditional timelines, shift societal patterns and change the arc of time. We hope as you make your way through this book, you see parts of your journey reflected in it. Take time to inhale and exhale: who knows where you will find yourself at the end.

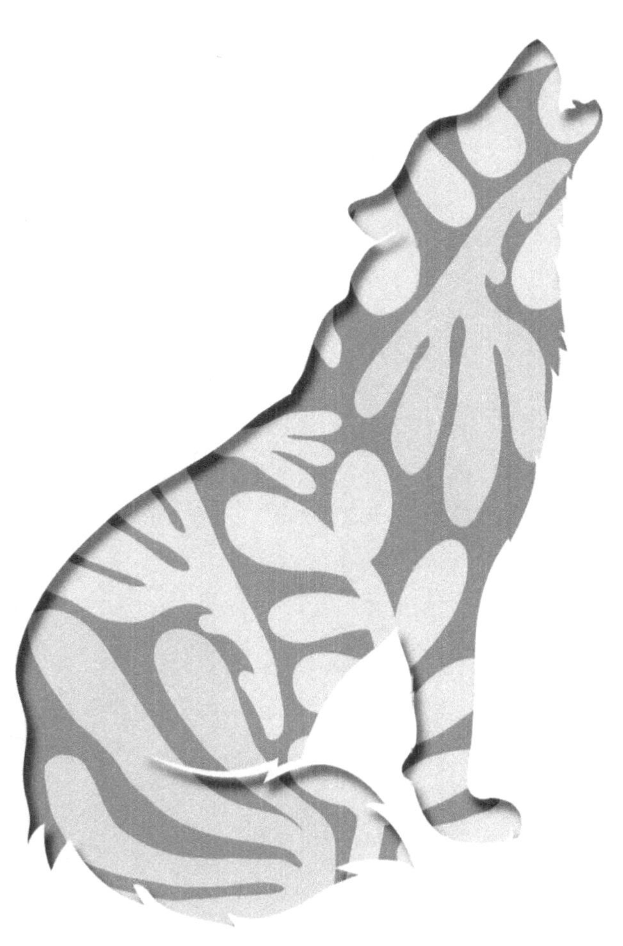

CHAPTER 1

THE RECLAMATION

Daniella Libri Elias

Dedicated to eleven-year-old Daniella,
who dreamed of one-day writing stories.
For all sisters, may we meet on fertile ground.

I was pulled back to the present with a forceful jolt – my body pulsating with unrelenting tremors. In the background, the sound of meditation music was gentle – a calm contrast to the new, yet ancient thrum of energy running through me. I tried to replay what had just occurred in an attempt to understand the magnitude of the moment. Everything had changed. I slowly paced, noting the light of the candles as they danced with flickers so intense it was like they, too, had witnessed my reclamation. They felt *them*; they heard *me*.

I followed a chord from my heart out of that room, trusting its guidance. Directing me towards the final task. In my mind it was all clicking into place, I knew what I needed to do. What I needed to say. And so as I anchored myself firmly in front of my love, feeling his curious eyes roam my messy hair and tear-stained face, I was grateful for his unquestioning silence. A patient pause in-between. He, too, could sense the power pouring from me.

A low howl of wind outside alerted me of their presence. They were still here. They would always be here. There was no turning back now and nowhere else to hide. However, in truth, I didn't feel fear. Instead, I welcomed their familiar energy, their wisdom. My Maiden, Mother, Enchantress and Crone revealed themselves through the vibrations around me, creating a solid wall at my back to hold me with what I was about to claim.

Raising my voice, not to yell, but to stand firm, knowing that these words were necessary, their meaning holding the weight of those who came before me and those who will come from me.

For the first time, I allowed myself to express without hesitation or uncertainty, and with the intention of being seen.

And so, I declared myself.

...

I always prided myself on being a good girl, doing just enough so that praise would coax my ego, but not too much, not pushing the boundaries enough to ruffle any feathers. No, that wouldn't be polite. To ruffle feathers meant to make others uncomfortable. To make others uncomfortable could lead to me being under the microscope, with whispers and judgment passed my way. Instead, I chose to be a great student, a good daughter, a responsible older sister – in the only way I knew how – to be quiet and to follow the rules.

I could achieve, of course, but not be lavish in the sharing of said achievements in case it would make others feel inadequate. I could speak my mind, but only if it didn't go against what everyone else in the room was saying. I could have fun, but not do anything that might embarrass myself. I could wear what I wanted, but only if it would be considered appropriate. I had to make sure to embrace all opportunities because my parents and immigrant grandparents had sacrificed so much to give us this privileged life. It was exhausting trying to keep up with it all. Trying to wear all the masks while covering the very essence of who I was.

Of course, it didn't stick.

Repressing parts of ourselves is never sustainable. But for a long time, that was how it went. I held such a deep fear about being a disappointment, even though I knew there was no evidence to suggest that I was. I felt confident within the strong walls I had built around myself, the mask placed firmly on my face. As long as no one could see what was beneath, I was safe. The real me was too much to fit into the mold society gave me. I was emotionally messy and opinionated. I felt too much, too curious about everything, and had the deepest desire to be free, to explore without limits.

The expectations I placed on myself were the highest of them all.

Daniella, do not mess up under any circumstance.

Daniella, do not say the wrong thing; you don't want to look stupid.

Daniella, just do what everyone else is doing and fit in.

Over the years, the mask became tighter and tighter, to the point where it felt like I was wearing another skin. I could no longer see or feel where the real me began and ended. On rare occasions, I would wonder where all of this pressure came from. *Why me? Why was I like this?* It was all-consuming. A burden I carried so heavily with me. For years, I believed the stories and repeated them in my mind, rejecting my individuality and accepting roles that I thought were what I was meant to do.

As women, we have done this for centuries. We have been silenced, shamed and made to feel less than. We have been underestimated, exploited and misunderstood. Our experiences have barely been documented. Our ritual selves, our powerful selves, our wise selves, all stuffed in a box over and over again, told to behave, told how to feel, how to act, how to react.

All of this has left us in a space of disconnect, we no longer know ourselves and our intuitive connection is limited. Mistrust is in our natural cycles and there are blockages right down to our sacral selves. When I step back, I see it is the essence of our femininity and the power we each contain that scares society because it can not, and will not, be controlled. It is potent magic, filled with healing waters. It is creation in motion with a heart-filled strength that could shake up the entire vibration of this planet.

It seems big, doesn't it? I guess that is why, for so long, so many of us have accepted a reality that is not our own. One that is not one we want. One that does not align with our sense of purpose, pleasure and joy.

Standing in front of my mirror, I reflect on the room around me. Outside the window, the shadows of the trees move in unison, a few long branches brushing their leaves across the glass. The moon is new, leaving a sky of black velvet to stretch as far as the eye can see. The only light sources are the candles around me and the dim glow bouncing off my open laptop.

Class is in session for Cycle School, but it has stretched late into the night, so a five-minute break is where I find myself. While I wait, my eyes land back on themselves. So brown, almost black, I have always loved my eyes. I thought them to be mysterious, although with age, I know that there is nothing mysterious about eyes – they are the portals to our truth. So much is shared through them. The way mine squint together when I smile, the lines that grace the sides of them, they tell stories of my laughter, of my lineage. Most of the women in my family have the same eyes. They connect us.

I notice how the light makes my dark hair look like silk and my olive skin glow. The hairs on my arms raise, an excitement in the air. My smile appears, lips closed like they know a secret. My eyes wandering down to my nose. This took some years to grow into. Once, it was attached to a string of insecurities, the heckles of other children calling me names. Now, I see it for what it is, unique, proud, unapologetic. In my reflection, I see myself, and I see flickers of my mother. I'm looking more and more like her as I age. I see my Nonna as well, I think it is my laugh, my cackle as it has become, where she comes out the most.

I can hear Claire, our teacher, in the background, prepping the music for the meditative journey she is about to take us on. I never thought at thirty-three years of age that I would be studying again. That I would be hitting the reset button on my life, yet here I am. I had to hit rock bottom in a career I had no passion for, and in spaces I created and lost my sense of self in. Lately, I had been unravelling from my heart space, trying to meet myself again, to get to know who I am, the me now.

I know all of my experiences, my learnings, and the people who have crossed my path have led me to this exact spot for a reason. Even if I don't know what that reason is. And so, I don't question what got me into Womb Work or what led me to study to be a Cycle Coach. I trust that learning more about our cyclic nature is exactly where I should be.

Claire's gentle voice instructs us to turn our screens off and get comfortable, to immerse ourselves in the meditative experience as best as we can. The theme has me curious, the plan is to meet our inner Enchantress, something I have never done.

I don't know what to expect as I lay down on my yoga mat, plopping the blanket my Nonna crocheted for me on top of my body, allowing it to cocoon me. A safe barrier, keeping me comforted and warm. Claire suggests we allow the experience to be what it needs to be. To flow with this journey towards the Enchantress. From what I have learned, the Enchantress makes up the energetic signature of the third phase of a woman's life cycle. Much like that of all archetypes, her energy is present within us all. She provides access and connection to the varied layers of the self. Embracing the universal wisdom, we hold within, forever guiding us through their experience and knowing. They reveal themselves through what we do and say, the things we crave and seek, and sometimes, they reveal themselves to us face-to-face, sharing without filter what we need to know.

Age-wise, the Enchantress could be anywhere from fifty to seventy years old. Her energy is a powerful, bold presence that is precise and knowing. She is intuitive, focused on the internal, and a big welcomer of change. The Enchantress holds strong and grounded energy and does not doubt who she is. There is a fierceness about her and a strong sense of sovereignty.

Is it nerves or anticipation that I feel running through me? This part of self is the part I know least.

Inhale deeply, exhale completely.

When I think about where I am in life right now, I have entered the Inner Summer, connecting very much to the energy of the Mother. Perhaps that is why I have manifested as the Mother version of self when I transport from the floor to a beautiful field of flowers. It is fitting. I may not have any children in the physical world yet, but the abundance of creativity that flows through my womb, the pull to give, to nurture, shows glimpses of the ever-flowing love that comes directly from her.

I look down at my loose white dress and smile, the wind blowing my hair, which is much longer and wilder than it usually looks, a few silver strands tucked in between. I hear the distant giggle of children, although when I look up, I can't quite see where they are – playing perhaps. That is when I notice a quaint cottage in front of me. Something about it feels like home. It looks warm and smells of cinnamon, and without going inside, I know it would feel like a hug. But it is not there that I am guided to, it is instead towards an ancient tree, its bark so textured and intricate in its natural detail. I allow myself to be lead. Intuitively knowing that opening the door, sitting right in its centre, is what I need to do.

It is after I have already stepped through the door that my conscious mind tunes into Claire telling us to venture through the door and down its spiral staircase into the home within to meet our Enchantress. *One step ahead.*

My staircase is made of wrought iron, beautifully detailed and sturdy. I run my hand along the textured rail as I walk down, and it is here that I notice my increased nerves. I can feel a craving for her, my Enchantress, like the Mother needs to be held by her for some reason. However, alongside that craving is also a tiny pull of resistance – uncertainty, almost fear, but not a scared fear. It is like my subconscious knows that the second I come face-to-face with her, she will shatter the final barrier around me.

Inhale deeply. Exhale completely.

My eyes grew wide as I reached the bottom of the staircase. Every part of the room feels like me. The lights are dim, with a roaring fireplace – crackling. There are big, comfy couches and books everywhere. I mean everywhere! The walls are lined with shelves. The floor has neat stacks upon stacks. I see dainty-looking teacups strewn around, markers of time well spent.

All I want to do is browse the impressive collection, choose a book, and curl up for a few hours, for a few days. Claire has other plans for us, pre-warning that our Enchantress is on her way. To prepare ourselves. Nervously, my eyes glance around the room, not knowing where she would be coming from. I stilled, trying to concentrate, listening for any change of sounds or a shift to the feeling in the air. Butterflies entered my stomach. *Why was I so damn nervous?* I gave my body a shake, closed my eyes, dropped my shoulders.

Inhale deeply, exhale completely.

I felt her. The moment she entered the room. She barely made a sound, yet her presence, that is what hit me first. I could feel how much space she was comfortable taking. I got the sense that I was very much intruding on her domain. Welcomed, yes. But only for a small amount of time.

When I open my eyes, the reflection I see startles me. Long grey hair tied back in a slick ponytail. A stern face, staring back at me with one eyebrow slightly raised. Thick-rimmed black glasses perched proudly upon her nose. It was this detail that stood out the most to me, at first. I found black frames were always too harsh for my face, adding a layer of fierceness I find intimidating, and yet, here she was wearing them.

She wore a crisp, white-collared shirt under a very soft-looking black jumper. Both are neatly tucked into tailored black pants. So severe, so unflinching. A certain level of intensity flows around her. If it was a colour, it would be silver. I wasn't scared, just taken aback. *Am I supposed to say something? Is she? Who starts the conversation here?* I didn't know.

Claire's voice in the background sounded distant, but I swear she said something like, 'Give yourself space to connect.'

How on earth do I do that? What am I supposed to express here? Shouldn't the Enchantress guide me? My throat felt tight. *Oh God, what do I say?* And right then, there was a flinch, a smirk that showed upon her face. And it was gone before I could take in her presence properly. *Could she hear my thoughts right now?* This was just too weird.

'Who are you?' She asked in a bored tone.

I was so confused, what did she mean? I know she knows who I am.

'Um... Daniella?' I responded questioningly. I didn't have any expectations of this meeting, but if I did, I am sure it wouldn't be this.

'Who are you?' She asked, firmer this time, pushing, waiting.

My voice was still uncertain, 'Daniella... Elias.'

She looked disappointed and frustrated with my response,

taking one step closer, her face closing in on mine, she said louder, 'Who are you?'

A deep buzzing filled the room, as goosebumps covered my arms. The intensity was unlike anything I had ever felt before. *She is me. She knows who I am. I don't understand what I am supposed to say.* My thoughts went to all forms of my identification: passport, driver's license, my library card. For goodness' sake.

'Daniella Elias! I shrieked, as tears filled my eyes. Why was I feeling so emotion filled. This was too much. Her judging gaze was too much. My heart felt heavy, like it would combust. My throat, scratchy.

'Who are you?' she pushed, eyes begging me to remember.

And so, I took a breath, exhaled loudly, and focused my attention within.

That's when I felt it.

I felt a red thread tugging my womb. I followed the thread and could see a line of women standing behind me. The maternal line. Generations of mothers, daughters, and granddaughters. All that came before me. I felt the tremor of their voices as they hummed in unison. Visions of me at every stage of life were sent my way. Every version of self, every part of me – my memories, my fears, my disappointments, my dreams. I felt every wish, every hope, every bit of love I had ever experienced. It rushed through me, quickly, all-encompassing and was completely overwhelming. I could see. In all of it, there she was – me.

'WHO ARE YOU?' Came out like a roar.

Then I broke. 'DANIELLA LIBRI ELIAS!' I screamed in her face. My body vibrating, tears exploding in waves. 'DANIELLA LIBRI ELIAS, DANIELLA LIBRI ELIAS.'

I collapsed into her arms from the wild force of energy running through me. I was exhausted and yet... relieved. Slowly, looking up at her face, I could see she had a knowing smile.

Her eyes crinkled, as she nodded, and said, 'Yes, yes, you are.'

I was pulled back to the room with a forceful jolt – my body pulsated. The meditation music gently playing in the background – a calm contrast to my new, yet ancient thrum of energy running through me. I tried to replay what had happened in an attempt to understand the magnitude of it all. Everything had changed. The candles danced with intense flickers, they too, witnessed my reclamation. They felt *them*; they heard *me*.

It made no sense and made all the sense in the world.

Everything I had been through, everything I had learned.

All I had sacrificed; all I had forgotten about myself. Somewhere along the way, I had gotten caught up in life and its fast-paced chaos and I had turned my back on who I was. I lost myself. I had allowed myself to be defined, directed and molded. My light dimmed. For so long, I had wished to have someone tell me that it was okay to be me, exactly like I was. I never realised that the only person I needed to hear that from was myself. That I could be my own permission slip.

My Enchantress wanted me to honour not just the person I am now but the person who got me here. She wanted acknowledgment, the complete embodiment of the most whole version of self. She encouraged me to reconnect with what I thought to broken. But I wasn't broken. I never had been, just a little lost. It was so clear now that all versions of me exist simultaneously. Daniella Libri, the version of self that held the fort for the years leading up to my marriage. This whole time, I thought I had to let go of her to be the version of myself that came with a new set of adult responsibilities when I changed my name to Daniella Elias. But they both were there side by side, both deserving of space.

A strong sense of knowing fired up from my womb and moved to my heart.

I noticed my reflection in the mirror, and my eyes locked firmly on myself. I stood up taller and prouder. With support of the archetypes surrounding me, I knew it was time to reclaim myself.

I am Daniella Libri Elias.

Daughter of Stelina Megale Libri.

Grand-daughter of Antonia Leonello Megale.

Great Grand-daughter of Carmela Tripodi Leonello.

In coming home to my truth, in embracing the messy flow of exploration that comes with returning to the self, I know that the healing I feel deep within my bones is sent through the red thread – healing those that came before me and those that I know are on their way.

I honour myself, and in turn, I honour us all.

ABOUT THE AUTHOR

DANIELLA LIBRI ELIAS

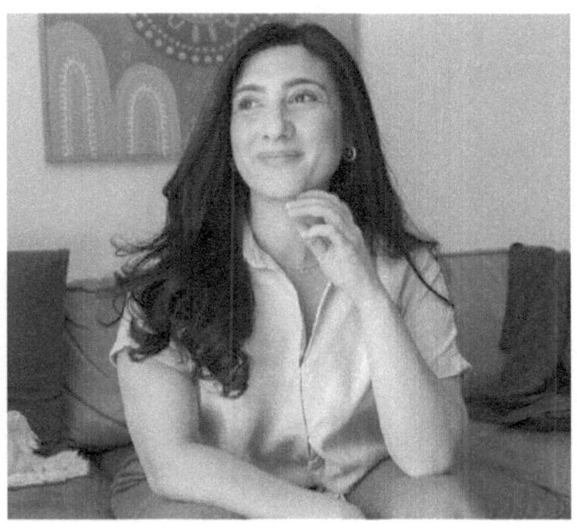

Daniella Libri Elias is a Certified Cycle Coach and intuitive guide. Daniella has worked with hundreds of women through her mission to reconnect them to the power they hold within. Her passion for understanding the unique characteristics of an individual's menstrual and cyclic experience, is what guides her work. For the past ten years, Daniella has prioritised her creative efforts through her businesses and feels most at home when holding women's circles, meditations and cyclic containers. She prides herself on the incredible community that surrounds her and is adamant that the women in her spaces are simply sisters, meeting on fertile ground. Daniella lives and works from her fairy-light filled home in Sydney. She spends most of her time with her nose in a book and a cup of cacao in her hand. She is an absolute pastry fiend and if there was a pain au chocolat sitting in front of her, she would refuse to share.

Access your free meditation to connect to the energy of your Red Thread, along with supporting journal prompts here:
www.daniellaelias.com/anthologia-meditation

thedaniellaelias
www.daniellaelias.com

CHAPTER 2

TRUTH OR DARE

Rose Mascaro

This story is dedicated to my mother,
who taught me that true love – and the truth – isn't always easy.
But both are worth it.

The game is truth or dare. Standing barefoot on your best friend's driveway, you can smell the damp of midnight eucalypts. A lamp on the street corner buzzes through the fog while seven or eight friends line up on the driveway to watch. He asks if you are ready. You thought it was wiser to go with dare because you hadn't even realised the game could come to this. He pushes your hair behind your ear and leans in, soft against soft, slipping his tongue against yours. He holds your face and raises the pressure gently as the countdown and your breath run out.

The dopamine ignites; a new engine is running through your veins. You drift home and all that summer you feel like you can see someone new in the mirror. You think about him often. You can't remember the colour of his eyes: only his long hair and the moonlight behind him. Soon your first period arrives and everyone talks to you about the taboos of sex but nobody ever talks to you about love. *Love*. Your mother yells bitter, throws plates, slams doors against your father. Four years ago there was *an accident*. Now your father can't climb the stairs to your parents' bedroom. He has crutches and crippled legs.

Back when it happened, you knew more than they thought you knew. Whispers, shadows and hurt spread like dishevelled newspapers in every corner of the shuddering old Italian house. Hospital visits, bright dark halls. Murmurs. Crying down the ward. Your big brother, so big he wore a suit and tie, asking your father – who lay stirruped and silent in the bed – *But Why, Why* – standing by the window, fists and jaw clenched, your father turned away. You held your dad's big brown hands, but when you looked closely you could see papery skin and purplish veins pulsing with morphine and psych meds. His eyes, oozing and wrinkled as his worn-out heart as he smiled his sorries at you. You closed your eyes tightly and delivered him your life-giving magic. And you always brought him back to life.

But always, *always*, there was a little shirt-pulling. A little voice. Perhaps it was that devil on one shoulder that all adults know, but no kid should meet. 'But why did he choose to leave *you* behind?'

As you stared out the window, and then at your dad, all distance and hollow eyes, you made a pact to yourself that you'll never be like all of them. *You, my dear, are light and sparkles and smiles... and all things nice...*

You held your dad's hand as he began to walk again. You

convinced yourself that it was your magic. The voice told you otherwise.

•••

All through your teenage years you think about the kiss. On the floor of your bedroom you read books of hobbits and teenage love. Your mother lays idle on her bed. She stares at the ceiling, glassy eyes full of tears and lost dreams. Your father is in rehab yet again. Meanwhile, you're busy conjuring up fantasy stories of stars and escape.

Mostly, you wait for the phone.

Eventually there are signs of relief in the shuddering old house. Your father gets better. His legs heal but he walks with a limp. The doctors get the balance of medication *kind of* right, but never *quite* right. He sits at the table every day, peeling a banana, opening the newspaper. 'It's OK, Bella,' he says to you in that soft Italian voice. Those sad eyes. He never says he loves you.

Just before you get too lost the phone rings again. You ride your bike as fast as you can to your best friend's house – your favourite place in the world – where dream catchers hang in every room and books are spread madly across Moroccan-style rugs. Afternoons are spent cutting up magazines and discussing lip gloss and movie stars. Here you can smile and breathe.

But then, of course, there's him. The older brother with the long hair – he hasn't forgotten the kiss. He waits for you in the halls with those dark eyes of want. He plays you his Nirvana albums when she's not around. He's obsessed with you: the innocent-sweet girl from the year below. You're in love with him: the pot-smoking bad boy from the year above. Once he says 'you scrub up alright' and you feel like you might one day *be something*. But he never makes you his girlfriend. He goes to the school ball with the most popular girl in his year – and that's the end of that. Many years later you catch a glimpse of him between the crowds of a nightclub. One day a blank stare in the aisle of Coles. By then he'd cut his long dirty hair into something respectable.

Before you know it, life sweeps past – studies, jobs, rent, promotions, engagements. Blink and you're suddenly married, mortgaged, living the dream. Trouble is, he has a phobia that reminds you of that hospital when you were nine. He tells you that you missed a spot on the kitchen counter. You feel a spark of hatred light up like a purple flame licking away at your heart and you wonder how you didn't see the signs earlier. You slide down the bedroom mirror, naked, startlingly-thin, biting the towel to keep from screaming.

When you sign the papers and receive the money you decide to become so visible that people will have to squint to look at you. This new gig would be a lifetime of celebration and forget. Your weekends become short dresses, glittering bars, cocktails in hand, $200 one night, $300 the next. Men's eyes devour you under the hot blaze of strobe lights. They leer longingly in your ears and dethrone you off the dancefloor podium. Always, they leave. Always, the comedown has you shaking and crying on the bathroom floor.

You wander through work days with horrific hangovers. You wonder about comfortable houses and comfortable suburbs and piles of uncomfortable bills. But remember – *remember* the blood that used to run through your veins? The blood that used to beat the sunshine pitter-patter of sparkle and warmth? Where did it go? You go to psychologists and spiritual healers, looking for a sigh of relief. A crystal pendulum. A set of tarot cards. A prescription.

Finally, you book the flight. The flight that will take you away. A psychic told you with cryptic confidence that you would find your heart again somewhere, elsewhere, *not here*. There's just one thing left you haven't tried and that's the tincture of travelling the world.

A tear slides down your cheek as you settle back into the vinyl seat. The buckle clicks into the realisation that you have no idea where you're really going. All you know is the number in your bank account which will give you one year. *One whole year*. The beauty, the blessing. The thrill of the fear. So many things you'd never done before, never seen. Your eyes fill once more as you think about your shaking parents hugging you at the airport. Your father, red-eyed and clutching your hand like it's the last time he'll see you. You'd wanted to tell him you know the feeling well.

...

Thirty-six hours later, belched onto the sandy streets of Mexico: *Your New Life*. Tumbleweeds of litter roll down a wide limestone street. A *Sol* beer truck screams past, dust rocketing from the earth. *One year here?* Mouth open and backpack strapped tight, you watch a moustachioed man walk past with a wide smile. 'Buenos!' All teeth and cheer, so vastly different to indifferent Australia.

As you walk into the main square, looking for *Where To Next*, a dog barks and a rainbow of colour hits your senses. Latin America, known for its multicoloured towns – their way of bringing life to urban living. You'd read in *Lonely Planet* that they paint their houses a new bright shade every Christmas. Just as Lilo collects photographs of fat people in Disney's *Lilo and Stitch*, you take a picture to start your collection of colourful old Mexican houses.

Later you slap your passport down on a hostel desk, shoulders sweaty and shaking from your backpack, and you're off. You're flying now. Pretty soon you're under the stars: a drunken night walking sandy streets in hot rain with someone from the hostel you've just met who says they love *being with you*. You want it to be love. But you know. *You know.* With the blow of a foreign breeze along your neck, you smile. It's a lonely smile. You wait for the hand to hold yours. It's been so long. You wonder what it feels like to be kissed again. You look up at the streetlamp that cuts through the night: always there, shining over your life at just the right moment. You smile and enjoy the high while it lasts, the warm ripples of lips against neck, the feeling of hands interwoven.

But soon you forget love and learn how to party harder, better. You learn the language of travel. You learn how to tell a cooler story. You learn to get what you want from locals who can't speak your language. Your life becomes one of *destination.* On the bus, travelling to yet another dropped pin on a map, you push your earplugs in hard to hush the cutting noise of your conscience. The relief to be nowhere and everywhere. To see the world through the gritty, grimy, fingerprint-stained windows. To place your cheek against the cold glass window, where dozens of other cheeks have rested as they've raised eyebrows to the sights of glorious mountains and fuzzy goats crossing roads in front of chicken buses.

Something has lit up your heart like a 24-hour streetlamp. The shirt-pulling voice is gone. You never knew it was this easy to be happy. If you had known this you would have left home years ago. But something in you knows that this is temporary; just another high that drowns out the voices – the voices that know too well the pain that sits within you. A pain that sits deeper than the dopamine dance that blitzes around your heart. Yes, those chemicals dance. From dopamine to cocaine, serotonin to valium, they all hold your hand in the dreamy waltz of the wounded. A dance under a foggy streetlamp and a kiss that you want to make last forever.

But this is temporary. *Temporary.* You must remember. You must. Remember. But it's so hard to when your next high fills you with something that feels so – so much like... so heart-shakingly close. And who cares whether it's real? *Good enough.* You wonder if it's the same for everyone on this route. You notice the weathered guys who lurk in the shadows of the beach every night, edging closer and closer towards bottle clinks and bonfires, bursting forth with a well-rehearsed travel tale at the peak moment of a shouty-drunk night, hopeful for a swig of beer – maybe even a new best friend. There's always a muttering of 'never go back, man, this is the dream,' though their eyes have long lost their shape and sparkle.

How long have they been here, you can't help but wonder?

You realise you are only here because of your bank account. You know that the dollars, at the moment, only make a small indent when withdrawn. So much money, it truly does equate to freedom and happiness. But one day you know that when you get to your last dollars you're not going to feel so happy anymore.

And then?

•••

Sunrise shears at your eyelids through a stained blue curtain. The song of far-off cockerels. You look around at the shapes of snoring travellers under sheets, thinking they look like a geometric puzzle. These people, these strangers, they've become your family. Beer breath and cigarettes; a hum of comforting vibration. You creep out of the dorm with your toiletries and inhale the wide green mountains, the ripe drops of water hanging from fronds. A little, brown-skinned Guatemalan woman with large eyes smiles at you. She is cleaning the bathrooms.

'Hola!' She has one large dimple in one smooth round cheek, just like you.

Half an hour later you are still standing at the sink while she cleans, chatting in the most broken of English and Spanish about all the great topics in life. The language barrier ironically doesn't allow for small talk. Simple words, big topics.

She asks you many questions, but you turn your attention back on her. She is happy; lucky here. A simple life with a family. She is younger than you but you can't help but feel she is older. Her body moves with wisdom and grace. You smile at her in the mirror and then at yourself, and you see something in your eyes – what is that? – Happiness? Peace? You dab on mascara slowly and deliberately, lengthening lashes, lengthening conversation. She wipes down the mirror and asks whether you have a family at home, but you know what she really means. *What are you doing here – don't you have children?*

'No. No necesito... Realmente no quiero tener hijos.' *No, I don't really want to have kids.*

She pauses, smiles, continues to scrub. You think of your dad. You hear the childhood voice again. The shirt-pulling.

She tells you to tell others how beautiful Guatemala is.

You tell her to enjoy her little boy who is waiting for her at home.

As you wander into the breakfast room before another day of adventures, you can't help but whisper on repeat the word she just said to you: *Tranquilo. Tranquilo.*

•••

That night you call. You can hear your father's happiness down the scratchy line. It's that sharp intake of mutual relief, when you know you're both alive. He chuckles and covers it up with small talk but you know he's shedding a tear.

'Dad, look, I need to talk to you about '91.' Breathing. Buzzing line. 'I think I understand now. And I know it's hard for you to talk about. I've been feeling a bit that way too, but I'll live my life now, K? I promise.'

His silence quivers with the words.

He's never said 'I love you', but you know.

ABOUT THE AUTHOR

ROSE MASCARO

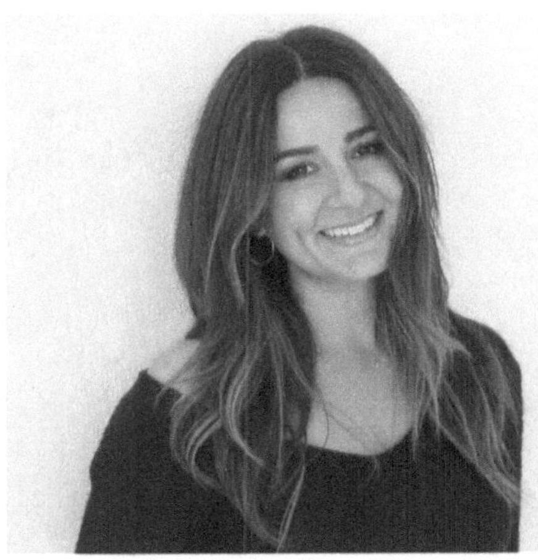

Rose is a writer, editor and teacher who is passionate about teaching others how to connect with their most authentic, heart-led words. She's the former editor of *Teen Breathe* magazine, Australia's leading mindfulness magazine for teens, and holds a master's degree in creative writing from UTS, Sydney. In a previous life, Rose spent over a decade as a secondary English educator in her hometown of Perth. Hearing the calls of her creative heart, she quit her job, travelled the world, studied yoga and meditation, and moved to Sydney to study her master's degree. She became a writer and editor specialising in fiction, travel, spirituality and lifestyle. In 2020 Rose launched *HeartWriting*, where she teaches powerful, authentic writing from the heart using a combination of literature, meditation, spirituality, and creative psychology. Her workshops are a perfect blend of spiritual connection and writing technique. Rose has written two books and has co-authored multiple titles for big names such as Lisa Messenger and Allura Halliwell.

heartwriting.com.au
www.heartwriting.com.au

CHAPTER 3

BELONGING

Kristina Garla

For my beautiful mum.
She has showed me how to live in this world with
a lightness of being and laughing heart.

pluck, pluck, pluck

She plucks at the skin at the top of her breast bone. Pinching at her heart centre, with her thumb and two fingers.

pluck, pluck, pluck

Her eyes are not quite fully closed. Perhaps this is her way of showing us she is still here.

The neckline of her nightgown does not interfere with the work of her fingers. Her right elbow rests by the side of her ribs as she plucks at her chest. Her other arm is flat against the side of her body. Her left hand, a dead weight in mine, is all flesh.

She does not squeeze my hand back. She does not flutter her eyes open. She does not respond to my whispers of love. She lays prone in the hospital bed. Propped up slightly by a pillow. A crisp, white sheet and waffle blanket covering her body from her breasts down. She is tucked tightly into bed, as only a nurse can achieve. But the sheet and blanket won't hold her down. When she is ready to go, she will. Leaving her body behind.

This is my Baba. She is seventy-two. A Lithuanian woman. A mother of two. A maternal grandmother of nine. The keeper of wisdom and laughter. The holder of traditions. The one who cooks koldūnai, cepelinai and soft caramel toffee. The woman who, at twenty-eight years of age, travelled with her beloved husband and nine-year-old daughter as cargo on a ship to Australia in 1949. Leaving behind her homeland. A refugee of war. Taking with her the ancient wisdom her bones had gathered from her ancestors, a small suitcase of belongings and a tiny stowaway in her belly.

At Bonegilla, Aleksandra was given card number 317. Serial number 100731. She stayed there for nineteen days before she and her husband, Mikalojus, my Duku, and her daughter, Irena, my mum, were transferred to the Department of Immigration Holding Centre in Cowra, New South Wales. At some point Aleksandra and her little family moved to Somers Camp in Victoria. In an unfamiliar heat of summer, she birthed her second daughter. In the gentle seaside air of Mornington, she and her family created their new home. My Baba worked as the much loved laundry lady in a house with sea views and sprawling lawns, owned by an Australian family who were building an empire from hosiery and lingerie. A family who welcomed her into their lives, opened their hearts and treated her like one of their own. When she wasn't working, she opened her humble home to the laughter and love of the Lithuanian community gathered there. Hosting parties and card nights galore. Music bouncing all the way down to the creek, which bordered the back of their property.

'Why don't you go home for some rest.'

I lift my head and watch as the nurse smooths the blanket a little.

'We will let you know if anything changes.'

I listen as her soft shoes pad out of the room.

Standing and leaning closer to give my Baba a gentle kiss on the cheek, something calls me to sing softly in her ear.

Do-ona no-obis pa-acem, pacem. Do-o-ona-a, no-obis, pa-aa-a-a-cem.

The words of a round sung in high school find my throat. The rhythm coming from deep in my belly. Latin words, their meaning foreign to me, and yet, their comfort wraps around us in this moment.

I gather my belongings from the pale blue chair. I pause as I leave to take one last loving look at my beautiful Baba lying there. In this moment, I witness her preparing to leave her body. Her last gesture here on earth. She is plucking from her physical heart, into the world, as much of her love as she can before she leaves. In this moment, I am twenty-two years of age. And I am not sure who I am or where I belong.

...

She lies still and cold, held by the white satin of her casket, and the silence in the room. The coldness of death has seeped into the walls. She, without her beating heart and laughing breath, is our grief's witness. Her hands have been placed, one over the other, resting on her ribs. Elbows by her side. She is dressed as if she could rise up at any moment, climb over the edge of her coffin and walk out the door. Shoes on. But she does not move. She simply lies there, as we take turns to sit by her side and sift through tender memories and tears.

I sit by her casket. Her skin is a shade of grey I have never seen and her hands are indescribably cold to touch. I close my eyes and feel the warmth of what once was. I too, leave my body. Somewhere else, I am thirteen. My Baba and I are sitting on the side of the bed in the bungalow where my family stayed for summer holiday visits. She is squeezing me in a tight hug as she sings Tina Turner's '*What's love got to do with it?*'

'Tina Turner is a grandma, and she can sing! Me too!'

We giggle all the way down to our toes.

My Baba is singing someplace else now. I look down at my hands as I blink my eyes open. I see the amber ring on my finger. My heart longs for more time with her alive. For her to return to her discarded casing before me. For a chance to have a closer relationship than we had. For her stories to shape me. For her stories to place me. For I am displaced. Because she had been. And I live in the hollow spaces between stories. A place devoid of belonging.

...

My sister and I watch her from the pool as she pushes the washing trolley to the clothesline. Barefoot, she walks with purpose and joy. As always. Her hair is short and her nails clipped neatly. Both are practical but beautifully stylish. Like her. She shakes out each piece of washing and pegs them into place. She is wearing a loose but colourful dress. It keeps her cool while bringing colour to the world.

She walks back towards us, walking on her bare heels at a quick pace. A nurse's pace. I am ten years old and this is my mum. She runs our household and the local private hospital with efficiency and love. She leaves no doubt of the never ending warmth she has to share with the world, with a smile so glorious and wide it can fill a room, or touch the sky. She leaves no doubt that she can get things done, because, she does.

Beautifully playful, she loves to dance, and sing. She does the housework on weekends to Elvis and Doris Day.

There is ginger beer and pickled herrings, which she has made, in the bungalow fridge. Later, she will collect them as she prepares our traditional Lithuanian Christmas Eve dinner. Twelve dishes, most of them garnished with freshly picked dill.

She leans against the tin side of the pool, and dips her fingertips in the water for a moment.

'Do you miss your mum and dad at Christmas time?' I ask her.

We'll see them soon enough. I'll call them after dinner.'

After sitting with her yesterday, and looking at old photographs, the shape of her is different to me today. I can still see the little girl with a giant bow in her hair sitting on the army jeep in Germany, and the young nurse on holiday, sitting on top of the shoulders of a man waterskiing on the water. I notice now in her hands the shape of the young mother who cheekily smiled back at me from the photograph, with one leg kicking out like she is about to dance. She is never still.

Watching her smiling up at the sun, I wonder why she settled her family so far away from her own. So far from those beautiful waves of the ocean.

She walks back inside, things to do. My sister and I float looking up at the sky, the water holding us at the surface as the sunlight dances around us. Birds swoop gently down to the pool water to briefly wet themselves a little, finding relief from the dry summer heat of this country town. I let myself sink under the water and rest there with my eyes closed. For a moment that lasts as long as my breath can hold me there, I belong.

...

The fine strands of her hair, which refuse to settle on her head, dance around her. The morning sun catches them and they make me smile. She has the energy of innocence as she dances through the door curtain into the sunroom. She looks up at me and smiles.

'What you thinking 'bout mama?'

'How much I love this house. How much it reminds me of my grandmother's, my Baba's house.'

'What was she like?'

'She was like... how your Baba is. Full of love.'

She smiles and the face paint wrinkles. It is Heritage Week at her school. She has asked for the Lithuanian flag to be painted on her cheek. Beautiful yellow, green and red. The same colours of the ribbons she wears in her hair. Ribbons from her grandfather's recent funeral.

This smiling delight, is my daughter. She is six. Last night over the phone she interviewed my mum, her grandmother, her Baba, for her school Heritage Week project. Together we captured the story of her Baba's childhood. We coupled it with a picture of my mum in tight plaits standing beside her first bike. We both notice the striking resemblance between my niece and mum.

'You have her smile too, mama.'

Her typed out story, and the story we are making in this

moment, land in the hollow spaces of my body. The sensation of displacement, which for so long I have carried, begins to dislodge itself. I am forty years of age, and for the first time ever, I begin to write my way home to belonging.

...

tap, tap, tap

She writes. From the depths of her bones the words come. Her fingers move over the keyboard as she allows the stories to spill from her soul. She delights in the mystery of where they fall. She writes one thousand words for one thousand days, dancing with her grief. She writes upon waking and hearing the whispers of wisdom that find their way to her as the gentle morning light changes the shape of the room.

tap, tap, tap

This is me. I am fifty-three. A second generation Australian woman, born to Lithuanian refugees. A mother of two. The keeper of wisdom and laughter. The holder of traditions. The one who writes her life alive. The woman who, at seventeen years of age, moved from a country town and left behind the sands of the river and family to arrive wide-eyed in Melbourne. I came seeking the ancient wisdom of my ancestors, carrying several suitcases of belongings, a tape recorder full of love songs and a heart full of dreams.

Sometimes when I write, my Baba sits with me. Although I cannot see her, I knows she is there. Other times I feel her dancing around me, wearing that makeshift toga from a party from long ago. A memory pressed into a photograph and a young child's mind. Mine.

We smile together, as myths from our Lithuanian heritage are rewritten. I reclaim something from the amber castle deep within the ocean and the tears of a mermaid, to build on a hollow past, long forgotten. I write about my younger self taking shape in the world, of being displaced, of searching for belonging. I write about my Baba, my mother, my daughter and me. I write about my family, plucked from their homeland and placed many thousands of waves across an ocean away. How, to begin with, their feet had difficulty finding the ground. How they were initially lost in a foreign landscape and a climate their bodies were not used to breathing. Lost in a language they could not understand. Displaced. I write about this loss of belonging becoming part of our bloodline.

My hands gently hold the piece of paper that once witnessed our family tree. It has faded over the years, and no one is here anymore to fill in the details for me. War took away records to connect me to my ancestry. The passing of days over time took away the people who remember. I am grateful I have, regardless of this fact, found them on my own. Discovered them in my body and breath. In the stories, which flow through me.

I tap from the keyboard of my computer the stories of my aching heart. Love. Betrayal. Life. Death. I come home.

Stories shape me. Stories place me. I belong.

...

What is it to belong? As a young child we tend to let belonging slip in-between us and others. It slides between the awkwardness of being a little different. As a teenager we will often grasp at it as we fiercely pretend we do not want it. As our skin gently wrinkles from days in the sun and laughter with our friends, we eventually find a sense of what it means to belong. We discover it in our very being. With every love we find and every loss we face. In our beautiful creations and in every goodbye we say. We find a deep sense of belonging in the stories we weave. In the life we lead. And in those we leave behind.

We all belong. Somewhere.

ABOUT THE AUTHOR

KRISTINA GARLA

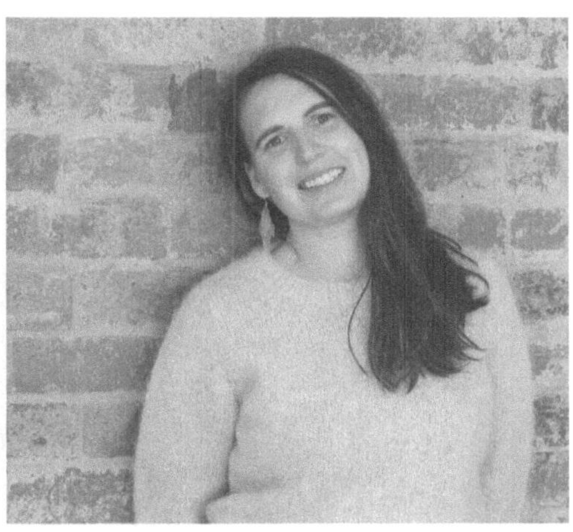

Kristina Garla was born on Yorta Yorta land to Lithuanian refugees. Her favourite childhood memories are running on the hot riverbank sand and eating her Baba's homemade koldūnai. Kristina has a special connection to where land meets water. She grew up spending a lot of time swimming in muddy creeks and rivers, beautifully clear bush streams, and the salty ocean. Kristina has been writing from the body for as long as she remembers; allowing stories to come through her, writing from the salt on her skin and sharing what her bones know. She loves the art of slam poetry and spoken word as much as she loves to write. She believes something exquisitely changes within us and around us when we speak our writing.

She lives on Wurundjeri Country and her voice holds space for people to heal through meditation, somatic and grounding practices, and her published writing. Kristina is blessed with two beautiful children, who keep her humble. She collects feathers; and magpies tend to hang out with her when she meditates in her backyard. Their song brings a beautiful sense of harmony and joy to her heart. Kristina peacefully insists for truth and believes in the guidance of love to change the world.

kristinagarla

www.kristinagarla.com

CHAPTER 4

LET'S BEGIN, THEN, WITH RAGE

Courtney Zerafa

Let's begin, then. Gather your pitchforks and your burning pyres. Your daggers need to be unsheathed, and your coats need to be billowing. You can picture it, can't you? The ferocious wind in your back as you stand at the foot of enemy lines; the aching pulse in your chest; the roar that demands more than this moment can give.

I am angry. I am broken. I am left hanging on the hook like a skinned cow at the butcher, and aren't we all? I am hungry. I am starving. I am aching to be seen. Aren't you as well?

We are monsters with our teeth cut out. We are wolves abandoned to howl at the moon. Call me ferocious and then say it's delicious when I wrap my limbs around your thighs. I am delirious, drunken, in agony. I want to crack open this voice box just to make it belch louder. I want to scream until my throat bleeds raw. Can you see how small I make myself? Can't you feel the boneless edges of my heart? I am sitting. I am waiting. I am reading my tarot and hoping for a sign. This darkened sword inside my rib cage needs warm flesh to strike. Lilith sits on my shoulder and whispers vengeance into my ear.

Here's the thing, I want to amputate my own temper. I want to strike it at the knees. This hungry fury keeps me ravenous and makes me beg. I want to scoop out my chest and not feel a thing. All this rage, all this frustration, only comes from grief. My anger is, of course, misplaced grief. Love that has been left out to bleed dry.

I only have two hands. Do you expect me to carry blades of anger in between my fingertips too? Shall I balance on a tightrope for you? Don't you understand, *I only have two hands*. We all only have two hands. I can only make a small fire. Bring me some sticks, some kindling, so we can build something bigger together.

Let's begin again, then. We should be strategic in our delusions. Let us never forget that female rage is a tightly bundled set of nerves nestled in the back of the brain. It is hidden in the subtle shift of our head and a quiet tremor. Women swallow their saliva and bow their head. Women point their arrows but wait for the right moment to release the arrow. Our hands fuse together as we can articulate a more calculated, honed response to injustice.

I do not wish to have rage furrowing beneath my flesh. I wish to live a gentle life. Poised and feminine and acute. I wish to wake in the mornings and pour my coffee strong and sit underneath a blazing sun and daydream the hours away. I wish to only dream of peace in a forest clearing filled with peonies. But instead, upon waking I must gather my bones and put on an outfit that will not catapult an onslaught of male attention but will still sing of my female charm. I must pour my coffee into a takeaway cup and sip it while I drive to work, where I will go and, a lot of the time, listen to men. One morning, as I sat at my desk and prepared for my day, a male colleague told me about how his mother once contracted a 'female' disease that impacted the functioning of her brain. He recited how now she cannot think straight, how she seems crazed and weak at the helm of her mind. The disease, it turned out, was a urinary tract infection that had spiralled into her kidneys.

'Men can get UTI's as well.' I told him.

He laughed, saying, 'I'm not too sure about that.'

In that moment, I probably could have pulled up scientific studies about male UTI's or told him anecdotes about a male colleague I once worked with who was in so much pain from a UTI he could barely think straight.

A female illness, indeed.

Instead, I smiled politely and told him I hope his mother feels better soon, all the while thinking that his voice-box – the one that screams of female weakness – was forged in the belly of a woman.

If you lift the lid off a female, what would you find? Calloused veins and steaming fingertips. Burnt edges and loveless memories. Inside you could find everything she ever hoped for that never eventuated. A warm home with a billowing fireplace, wood always gathered by its side; tilted lampshades with ivory patterns; laced curtains and a full vase of sunflowers.

What is it to be a woman in a man's world? What is it to have to falter and recalculate your steps? Must we always tread carefully?

On any given Saturday night, I will gather with my friends,

and we will read our tarot. We search the future for answers. We look up at the stars and wish for answers. We command our days, spend time in boardrooms or classrooms, we run households, we hike torturous mountains. We are always seeking. Why? Our rage sits beneath it all.

Women wave their white flag before the battle has begun. We want the peace before we want dead soldiers at our doorstep. We do not want to have to stay up late and wait. We do not want to write letters that will never be delivered.

Our rage is coaxed out from our throats in an overwhelm. Men will bellow and belch and yell. They will slam their hands on tables and slam the door as they walk out. Women will stretch their limbs and pray. Women will put away the knives that have been left on the kitchen sink and do the dishes. They will tidy the living room and turn off all the candles.

But old habits die screaming, and a woman never forgets the fire they used to burn our bodies. Our precious skins can recall the burning of flesh, and we will either cower at the flames or stoke them. Let us never forget that women can throw punches and rip the skin off an angry man if they need to.

Working in a prison reserved for males, I have felt the eager violence men feel. The way they see it as a duty. The blood on their hands serves as a badge of honour. Their anger can always be justified. Their burning flames work as a signal for a job well done. Some days, I leave work tired from holding the anger of men and giving them the space to make their vicious visceral. If a woman takes a knife out on the sidewalk, she is a psychopath. If a man does the same, he is defending himself. When I tell a coworker that I am considering working with female inmates instead, she casually tells me females are much worse than men.

A woman's anger bubbles until it has no place to go. Then the fury is unleashed.

Let us look to popular culture then. There is a slew of females scattered across our vision who portray the ghastly and the angry and the almighty. Jessica Jones, Harley Quinn, Aelin Galathynius. Killers who are mad in their rage. Cleopatra was a Queen but many only recognise her for the love affairs she had with male leaders starting wars. The angry women we can admire are often left lonely, or weak at the knees for a man, or die in their own dismal glory amidst a casket of flames.

Princess Rhaenyra Targaryen, the female Queen in House of the Dragon, is consistently portrayed as a woman fuelled by scorn. Even when she is left aghast by grief, her actions are coloured by her rage, her envy. Female friends become enemies, children are murdered, men are squandered, and it is all portrayed as misguided female rage and ambition. The death in her wake is the making of her reign.

Is a woman chasing ambition only angry?

I wonder if our anger must always serve a higher purpose. Can we be mad without obvious cause? Let us begin again and wonder, honestly this time, why our fury must always be portrayed as crazy instead of guided. Cleopatra knew exactly what she was doing, and so *we* must always know what we are doing.

What is it to be an angry woman? How tight must my shackles

be before my wrists start bleeding? When they do bleed, I am the one blamed for the trail of red. We are left to trudge through the grime forever, only ever feeling specks of sunlight in between the greying skyscraper streets.

When I am angry, I am uncontrollable. I cannot hold it all in until it bubbles over. My bubbling over happens before anything else. I wonder if I have spent so much time around masculine rage that it has seeped into my soul. The rage feels like I am already full to the brim with feelings. I wake and am angry. I sleep and am angry. I want to let go of all the anger but when I do it comes out in tall wisps of smoke that choke everyone. As a woman, it seems impossible to feel the entire roar in our chests without accusing yourself damned for not being a tomb of peace.

On a different morning, the same male colleague with the mother fallen to a UTI asks me what I am currently writing about. I tell him, casually, that I am writing a piece about female rage. At this, he scoffs.

I am restless. I am unsteady. I am sitting with fists of fire that turn to ash before I even have the chance to speak.

There is a skewed cadence about growing up. We are told that we have learned to regulate our emotions only when we can be calm in situations that could rile our bones. Am I forsaken when I cannot regulate? Should I instead smile when I am offended? Should I retort back to the sexist comment or is it more wise to let the comment go unanswered? It is not so easy to remain the butt of the joke for an entire lifetime. It is not so easy to be the graceful woman in a world of towering patriarchy.

What is a woman's rage if not overwhelm? If not the feeling that everything is slipping through our fingers. I let them take my body. I let them tell me what to think. I let them scoff. I bake them glorious dinners. Still, it is not enough. Still, I want to take a boxing class just to know what it feels like to hit back where it hurts. Still, I want to learn karate so that when an angry man purples my skin, I can at least try to fight fire with fire. Still, I watch the news and wince at the constant stream of news stories that report of a woman killed by a man who has an anger uncontrollable.

Angry men have circled me my entire life. I have been the gazelle amongst lions. I have fled the scene. And, when my ex-partner would yell, I would yell back. I would swing back. I would be the almighty lioness protecting her cubs.

One night, when he wanted to hurt me without bruising my flesh, he took our cat and dangled him off the side of the 17th story of our apartment. In that moment, all rage left my bones and I ran to cradle the cat from his grasp. Anger dissipates when a threat is near, then. For a woman, the need to protect outpaces the need to fight. Who wins in those stories when the woman must bow in order to save a life? A man and his anger know no end, but a woman can feel the end of the rope and pulls it back toward her when she needs to. Rhaenyra Targaryen did. Men with their grazing fists and aggressive tendencies have killed women for millennia, so why is it women's rage that is condemned?

We are taught that our desire is villainous, that our rage only lends to further bloodshed. That Eve bit the apple and now our entire line must be admonished. We must sit out eternity, pleading for our sins to be forgiven, because the serpent played with our might and we succumbed.

Lilith is the angry woman. The martyr of the beastly ones. She is the one who would not bow to a man, and now she is the god who is worshipped by those who have forsaken their matronly roles. The worship of Isis is left in tatters for us to slowly uncover because a woman who holds power is, for some, a scary idea to swallow. Psyhke killed in the name of love. Athena condemned Medusa because she was jealous, upset, angry. So many stories of a woman's anger are consistently the arc of love gone wrong, washed in jealousy and misconstrued hope or lust or merciless envy.

I wonder, when we are angry, are we upset that our love – our love that is pure and matriarchal and true – has been misconstrued and laid to waste? Are we angry *or* are we tired that our limbs are forever searching for a place to rest? Do we think our legacy will be buried if we do not shout our treason from every rooftop with a view? We are waiting on the battlefield, pitchforks at the ready, before the end has a chance to eat us whole.

If we put our hands together and build a fire they can't tear down, we may not have to sit with such aching fury in our chests.

Let's begin, then, with rage. Let's never put our knives down and pray that our overwhelm is never admonished. Let us have the guts to give our overwhelm a clearing to screech into; open our mouths so wide that our anger has the room to pour out. Our grief needs a place to rest, so let's find a space in the forest and build a fire that cannot be drowned with water. The wind is at our backs. Lilith is on our side. It's a battle that may yet be won.

ABOUT THE AUTHOR

COURTNEY ZERAFA

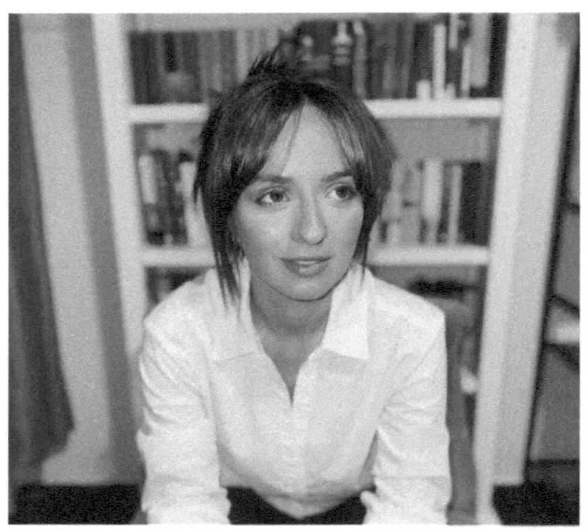

Courtney Zerafa is a freelance writer who lives just outside of Sydney, Australia. When she isn't living out the consequences of her gilded desire, she is tending to her multiple fur babies and human baby. You can spill your heart out to her via Instagram, or you can let her spill her heart out to you on her blog.

Instagram @ korts__
www.kortspivot.wordpress.com

CHAPTER 5

SCARS OF OPPRESSION RUN DEEP

Beryl Crosher-Segers

To my mum,
who bore the weight of oppression with dignity,
nurturing our resilience and teaching us the true
meaning of strength.

I had a typical childhood in Cape Town, South Africa, during the sixties. I played outside from dawn to dusk with family and friends from the neighbourhood, and we lived in complete ignorance of the wider world.

As I grew older and listened to Dad's stories and those of my high school teachers, I realised that I had grown up beneath the oppressive shadow of the community's longing for lost properties, family divisions and resettlement. The gathering of women, and their stories of domestic abuse, alcoholism and overcrowding, coupled with the aroma of particular dishes, take me back to a time when our community's terrible reality cast a shadow over my innocence. My upbringing in a segregated community with a shared racial identity was moulded by this existence, and it would eventually become a significant part of my life's journey.

A greater awareness developed when I started college in the 1970s. Like a lot of young people, my then boyfriend, Chris, and I took pleasure in our celebration of life through music and dance. We dressed in the typical flower children attire of the time – colourful vests, bell bottoms, afro hairstyles and Chris had the rebellious sideburns known as 'lamb chops' to establish his early manhood. The sixties and seventies were very much influenced by meaningful lyrics, 'make love, not war' slogans on T-shirts and peace sign necklaces. While South Africa enforced an international media blackout and books and music were censored, DJs introduced us to banned music and books and newspapers circulated underground.

In this essay, I want to describe the importance of story in our lives. The stories of survival we shape for ourselves. The stories we tell our children to preserve family history and heal ourselves and remind a new generation of what went before them. Rest assured, we are all characters in our own stories, and we can shape our plotlines so that a positive message wins the day.

My own story has its roots in apartheid-era Cape Town, South Africa. The unpleasant triggers from that time continue to affect me, but I have developed a resilience to move beyond the wounds of my past.

Growing up there, I didn't know there was a richer life behind the bushes, an alternative dimension on the other side of the railway line where white children were living privileged lives. I was oblivious. As a child, I even thought apartheid was normal.

But age soon brought a jolt of awareness.

After the release of my memoir, *A Darker Shade of Pale*, I was approached by a postgraduate student who wanted to make a short film about my story.

Part of the project involved filming my ninety-year-old mother, who lives on the New South Wales Central Coast. She was asked about how life had changed for her when the apartheid laws were legislated in 1948. I had brought along two of the original wooden signs used to separate us from other races in public places. We used them as props for the film. These signs, which said, 'whites only' and 'non-whites only' had been displayed on train carriages and painted on benches on the platforms and at entrances to buildings.

To say I was unprepared for Mum's reaction is an understatement. Mum had always been the calm in the storm at home whenever my father raged on about oppression. She remained laser-focused on educating us and working day and night to keep a roof over our heads. For some reason, I thought that she was accepting of her classification as a second-class citizen.

The plan was to film Mum paging through my book, *A Darker Shade of Pale* and to ask her some questions about her life back in South Africa, and how her life has changed since moving to Australia forty years ago. Instead, she gripped my book and refused to touch the wooden signs. She demanded that we remove the relics from her sight. Water would have frozen instantly when the words poured out of her mouth.

'I remember the day when life changed for us,' she said. 'I was eighteen at the time. These signs appeared out of nowhere.'

'But didn't you know that things would change?' I asked.

'No one talked about it,' Mum said, staring at my unopened book. 'My mother was a simple woman, always in the kitchen, cooking and cleaning. My father was always out working.'

My maternal grandfather, Emmanuel, was born in Lisbon, Portugal. He married my grandmother, Fransina, of Mozambican descent shortly after he arrived in South Africa and before the segregation laws were imposed. The Immorality Act forbade interracial marriages. His marriage to my grandmother was a demotion and forced him to live in an area designated for non-white people. This changed the trajectory of his future compared to other Portuguese immigrants, who were classified as white.

'The boere (Afrikaner police) stopped us from crossing the bridge to get to the other platform to catch the train,' continued my mother. 'They called it their bridge and herded us like cattle down the side of the railway line to the train crossing about 200 metres down, to get to the other side.'

The filmmaker stood behind his camera, unsure whether he could film. The wooden signs lay discarded behind the chair.

'Why didn't you ever tell us this story?' I asked.

'I was too busy taking care of all of you, working day and night and supporting your sick father, to think about this,' she said. 'You know, I haven't thought about this for many, many years. I am ninety years old, and these pieces, these rotten pieces of wood with those words, probably painted in some railway workshop by people who thought they were superior to us, brought back all those memories.'

I felt responsible for awakening Mum's trauma. My stomach churned. Having written my book and spoken about it at length in book talks and interviews, I felt that the sting had been removed from my past.

Driving along the Pacific Motorway back to Sydney, the wooden signs lay face down on the seat next to me. I thought about my own experience of the railway station and the signs. I didn't want to think about it. I wanted to distract myself with the stunning views over the scenic Mooney Mooney Bridge, but I simply couldn't stop the memories from flooding back.

I was eighteen years old when I began to grasp the depth of the inequality that I had been born into. It was when I first saw how family, friends and many of my fellow citizens were trapped in a toxic system. For the first time, the realisation that we were stuck in a life of poverty and degradation stared me in the face. While Dad had drummed into our family that we were just as good as anyone else, white South Africa was organised around telling us a different story, as loudly as it could. Its plotlines went beyond words to actions of cruelty and subjugation.

We were brainwashed into accepting that being chased off beaches and benches not allocated to us was normal. We grew up walking to our train carriage down the end because the signs on the doors barred us from sitting with white people.

We were brutalised and dehumanised every single day. We

grew up with an inferiority complex being drilled into us by South Africa's powerful, white storytellers, who said: 'You are not the same as we are.'

They forced us to be spies in our own lives.

Always on guard.

Always feeling we must aspire to be like white people to be successful.

When you're forced to strive to be someone else to survive, you can lose touch with who you are.

The sound of my phone ringing jolted me back to the present. My son's photo popped up on my screen, but I couldn't answer. Through my tears, I turned up a Crowded House song. I would call Michelin back later.

As I stepped through the front door at home, Chris said, 'Michelin called to say that Alexander is sick. They might take him to hospital if he doesn't improve.'

'Oh, that must be why he called earlier.'

A wave of exhaustion fell over me. The day had been emotionally and physically draining and soon I fell into a deep sleep. The ring of my phone jolted me awake around 6.00 am.

'Are you awake?' I heard Michelin's voice followed by a long yawn.

'I am now. How is Alexander?'

'We're at the hospital. They admitted him last night. Lisa stayed home with Mia and Joshua.'

'OK, we'll head over to see him as soon as your dad wakes up,' I said, trying to keep my voice calm.

On the drive over to the Northern Beaches Hospital, Chris and I talked about how Michelin suffered from asthma at the age of three, the same age as Alexander was now, and how our experience of taking him to hospital cemented our decision to return to Australia.

One winter's night, in 1984 in Cape Town, Michelin suffered an asthma episode. The paediatrician advised us to bring him straight into the hospital, where he operated a private ward for his patients of all races. But he wanted to examine Michelin first to assess whether he had to be admitted. Gesturing to follow him, he entered the white side of the public hospital in search of a bed. The hospital staff refused us entry and told the doctor to use one of their beds on the 'coloured side' for our son.

Chris and I were enraged, but we were more focused on Michelin's ability to breathe.

We were told to go to the other side where they treated coloureds. They did not want his little body to touch their white sheets.

Mum's story and all that had developed from that was trapped in my psyche. I realised that trains played a pivotal role in my exposure to the brutal apartheid era. It was on a train platform that we were confronted with our confused five-year-old daughter, Sasha, who wanted to get into a train carriage marked for white citizens.

The psychological damage of racism and discrimination is

lasting, and I have no doubt many of you bear your own personal experiences of struggle.

Because of *A Darker Shade of Pale,* people now ask me what I see as racism. Yes, it exists on a spectrum, but when it comes to apartheid, I must be crystal clear.

Apartheid was not 'a bad thing'.

Apartheid was horrific.

It was depraved and dehumanising. It was evil, ugly and violent. It was indefensible in every way.

Apartheid was a crime against humanity.

Remembering the pain and horror of those memories can shock us into a renewed awareness.

It jolted me into a heightened awareness of my surroundings. This was precisely what I experienced when I entered the hospital ward where Michelin sat cradling Alexander, who was on the nebuliser.

I scanned the private room and couldn't help but notice the clothes and shoes scattered across Michelin's unmade folding bed and the toys strewn all over Alexander's bed.

The moment the nursing staff entered to check on him, a wave of unease washed over me. All I saw was white skin. I nervously tidied the room. I didn't want them to look at us through the lens of our skin colour. I thought that the state of the room could tarnish our image in their eyes. My dad's voice rang in my ears, him saying, 'We are good people, just like anyone else.'

'Mum, Mum – stop! What are you doing? Michelin asked.

'I'm just cleaning up before they come back,' I said.

Michelin smiled and cradled Alexander in his arms.

'Relax, they come in here to check on Alexander,' he said. 'Not to do a room inspection. And, besides, there are thirty-five other rooms for you to clean if you feel so inclined.'

Triggers. They never leave us.

These feelings can be awakened when we least expect it.

Having dedicated 35 years to public service, I am proud of the part I play in serving our community. Working in a culturally and linguistically diverse community has broadened my perspective of the challenges people face. My hijab-wearing colleague told me about an experience she had a few years ago at Central Station. She was on the platform when a public announcement informed passengers that Australia was on high alert for terrorism. Passengers were urged to report any suspicious behaviour or packages left unattended. She told me that she felt as though thousands of eyes were fixated on her. She couldn't shake the feeling that her presence, marked by her hijab, had inadvertently made her a focal point of attention. She experienced the complex dynamics around identity, anxiety and perception in our community.

These scars of oppression run deep, shaping our identities and interactions in profound ways. That is why it is important to document our stories – not only to record the atrocities but to show how we survived while continuing to live with our trauma.

ABOUT THE AUTHOR

BERYL CROSHER-SEGERS

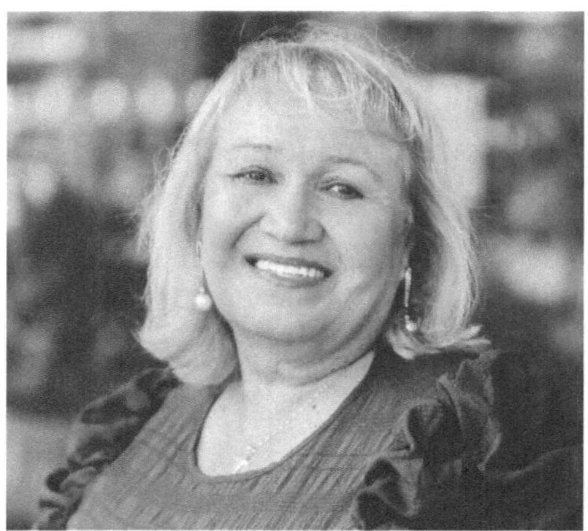

Beryl Crosher-Segers is the author of a bestselling South African memoir about life during apartheid, *A Darker Shade of Pale*, as well as *Behind my Smile: The True Story of an Author, a Broken Spirit and a Healer* and *Living with Purpose*. In her writing debut, she tells the story of her determination to rise above her earlier life of inequality and injustice.

Beryl and her husband moved to Australia in the 1980s in search of a better life for themselves and their children.

Through a long-held love of the arts, she established One World Community Arts Network, a community project celebrating cultural diversity through music. Through her commitment to previously disadvantaged artists from her town of birth, she started her own events company, C Major Events. Beryl's previous experience is in administration in government. She is also impassioned by fundraising for worthy causes.

A highly-regarded community representative, her awards include the Celebrate Africa–Australian Captain's Award for service to the South African Community and a Jo Wilton Memorial for Women, a human rights award, from the University of Technology in Sydney.

She started dabbling in lyrics in 2020 and released her first song *Colour Blind* in December 2020. Other song releases followed, including *Grace*, *Pieces of Dreams* and *Look At Us Now*. These songs are currently receiving high numbers of downloads. She is also currently writing her fourth book, a psychological thriller called *Silent Tracks* and completing another memoir.

Beryl holds postgraduate qualifications in Creative Writing from the University of Technology.

berylcroshersegers_author
www.berylsegerschronicles.com.au

CHAPTER 6

CURSED GIFT

Hannah Bishop

For the girls,
and for Hollie –
my one and only goddess.

A wince of discomfort as nails dug into the skin by her ankle bones. The night was eerie around them, save for the cascading wails and cries of the woman at her feet. Months later, she would recall this moment and see the brutal parallel as Medusa grasped at her legs, hunched and weeping, whispering prayers to the sandalled tops of her feet. Begging, pleading, apologising unjustly as the rust-stain of her handprints dried along the skin of Athene's calves. She would scrub the blood clear a dozen times over every day, but still feel the woman's hands on her. She would feel her hands, her forehead, the hot of tears, the humidity of whispers, but she would not recall the image. Stoic had she been, to stare ahead and past the pillars of her temple to the quiet of her city instead. A city she had just won, a blasphemer who had desecrated her honour, and to show she was worthy of the name she gave, punishment had to befall.

Like a blade to a traitor's neck, like sacrifice to a favour, like a curse to an innocent.

Because it is never the guilty who are damned.

...

This beauty had been turned into monster the moment she had defiled a goddess's temple. That was what Athene had been told before she laid down her punishment. Guards held the woman back from her, their eyes only watching from their peripherals as Athene had cast her curse. Dishevelled locks turned to writhing snakes, her sweet teeth that had left splits in her lip grew to uneven tusks and fangs, eyes of the ocean clouded over and filled with the splatter of fresh blood. Her final stroke were the tears that froze where they lay on her skin, sharpening and turning to scales.

'Don't you see it?' Medusa had hissed. Lips smacking together in her attempts to articulate her words around deformity and emotion. Athene closed her eyes, unable to bear the scene any longer. '*You are no different.*'

Silence returned to the temple, a more harrowing sound than to have the night cracked open with suffering.

Athene nodded, the gorgon's head covered, and she was dragged away. Taken to be scattered like ashes on the wind. Taken so that Athene could dust her hands of the beast and continue with her immortal life. Take the praise, accept the gleaming pride of her father at having been as ruthless and conceited as he, return to solitude on her rocky peak to watch the world. The gods had been so impressed of her curse, the fine detailing of its detriment, but now it had shown to be more of a bother to the mortals than the gods could enjoy.

How was she to know there would be consequences for her actions? It was hardly ever a sparkle in the minds of gods. She doubted that even her father housed the word in his vocabulary. But of course, now she did because of mortal man's inability to take no for an answer, and so they were dropping like flies in the stoney wake of her cursed creation. It was usual for gods to enjoy their chaotic creations, but she could not when what happened instead drove her fellow Olympians to lengthy bouts of complaining. Their temples were overrun with wailing wives or weeping mothers at the loss of yet another man-cum-statue.

It would have been so easy for her. The grandest game of the hunt, the likes even her sister would envy. It was a possibility she revelled in. The thought of taking her strides in the pitiful wake of her creation, just to be the one to fell another blow to her was thrilling. Shivers down her spine, palms that itched to grasp and take, lungs that yearned to breathe in the sweet salt of sweat that dripped in fear.

It was a shame, then, that a prophecy had been murmured into the ether. The boy called Perseus had a fate resting on his shoulders with which she could not interfere. It seemed unfair – a half-breed would take her claim of victory from her because of the crazed words wound up in the prose of prophecy.

He, the son of king and princess, will be the one to lead the hunt and bear the fatal weapon.

Snivelling little Perseus would be the one to kill the gorgon. This beast of her creation, which shattered lives and statues, if rage and a tight fist followed her stare. Athene had dashed a pebble or two across a lake as she had wended the path once trod by the gorgon, would hear the rage in her screams when she cradled the pieces of what Medusa's power could do. Screams that rode in her blood like the ichor that shimmered within, that grated in her ears like the vice of her jaw. The boy would kill the gorgon, and there were two splitting veins in which Athene could carry her disappointment to in the fact.

Perseus was the one to lead the hunt, and it was true. There was nary a soul at his heels as he pursued the gorgon. But Athene was not one for heels, not since the debacle that took place in Troy. Instead, she was at the helm, as was her preferred position. Hermes had gifted the boy his sandals, and she was commanded by her father to bestow her shield to him as well. The reflection of the gorgon was not one with the power of her full stare. Athene wondered or not if it were true, or just a hopeless wish to make the prophesised one feel more confident in his venture.

Yet, she waited. Her path took her deeper into the forest, and she noticed as the silence ebbed in, another's steps echoed hers. Beneath the speckled moonlight, she turned and stood still. Perseus approached, his face contorted, eyes wide. When he saw her, he puffed his chest and let his brows sink to shadow his eyes. An accentuated bow for show to only the audience of gods that would hear the story later, and Athene schooled her features to neutrality.

'Chosen Perseus, the prophecy bestows on you a great honour.' Her voice was monotone; anything else would have come across facetious.

'Goddess Athene,' he said, voice showing his youth. 'You are no different than mighty Zeus described. Foreboding, powerful...' his voice turned to an irritating hum as his words echoed in her brain.

You are no different.

Medusa's last words to her before her voice became garbled by her tusks and sorrow.

Perseus was still rambling. Platitudes but Athene was unlistening and uncaring. He was making a droll afternoon bleed into evening without her consent to its boredom. 'Stop,' she commanded. The boy did, and after a beat, clenched his fist and shot his chin skyward, though his neck was blotched with unseemly crimson. It seemed pointless to delay the prophecy, and so she held out her shield to him lest he remain stoic and unmoving for any longer. His arm slid into its backing, and he was pacing backwards to swing it around a few times. For what purpose, the goddess did not know. She only looked down on the mortal as he did so, imagining it was what children did on birthdays with some shiny new toy.

A child. A child would get in her way.

'I bid you thanks,' he said, as she had still spoken no word regarding her shield that was strapped to his arm. Heat rushed to her chest as he began to stride away, the muscles of her arms tensing as she watched his minor one's strain to carry her shield in all its weight. But she could not do a thing.

That was it then. She was to turn and leave, let Perseus enact the prophecy and claim his victory as Athene returned to the vacuous halls of Olympus. But a nagging ran through her body that called for her to follow, to watch to the end of Medusa's life and the pitiful show the boy would put on to achieve it. Like she had watched her heroes fall before, or the gruesome gravity of war be tossed from city walls to crash into burning depths, Athene was compelled to witness her creation's demise even if it could not be at her hand.

With each step Perseus took, Athene matched it. Her fingers twitched by her side, curling, and pinching against each other as the evening befell them. Silence wrapped around her like a shroud, her own breath the crispest sound to penetrate it, and somehow the most unnerving. The boy's shadowy figure appeared before her, too close, and she paused in the concealment of a tree. In her realm of quiet, she watched as he turned, seeming to have become aware of something filling a crack in the night. She moved her head to stare far deeper into the thicket of trees to where he was staring and found a distant shape, barely noticeable and nothing more than a jagged rounding of boulders. Perseus must have thought it a spooked animal since vanished, or the ghosts rumoured to haunt the forest coming out to play and bewitch in the twilight.

He turned away, proceeding in his naïve search. Athene, however, kept her eyes on the figure. A long beat passed, her eyes screaming to blink or at least move to see where the mortal had gone. But at last, movement.

A shifting wave around the figure's edge, soft curves that sharpened and danced, then became strands of weaving magic. Coils that reached in every direction, tips finding each other in rendezvous then parting ways to feast on the sweetness of cool air. Athene stared in rapture, eyelids blinking furiously but taking it all in. The figure moved, arched, and stretched as she stood. Her coils came back to her, before darting out again. Shoulders hunched, suddenly feral, she turned her head in the direction of the boy.

As the beast moved, long legs elegantly carrying her form through the undergrowth, the night illuminated her. In this being, the goddess saw the creature she had created, and how it had evolved into something greater than even she could have imagined. A monster in every sense of the word if only just to survive. A gorgon only in curse but growing into herself as she moved. As Athene stepped to follow, she saw Medusa grow close enough to spy Perseus, then turn. Stupefied by the move, Athene stopped. She watched the gorgon dash in small, structured steps of silence that carried her across the forest floor in the opposite direction of the boy hunter.

Eyes flicking between the two other figures in the forest, Athene at last watched the trees swallow Perseus. A sensation swelled in her chest, rolled through her ribs to pull at her shoulder blades as if she might spur wings. Medusa continued her skitter across the earth, bringing her closer to where the goddess hid. When her escape lured her close enough, Athene stepped out in a flourish of sudden wind and shuddering branches. The gorgon came to a halt, stumbling to the ground in the goddess's might, but used her only defence as she did.

At the last moment, Athene realised her mistake and panicked her eyes to close. A breath too late, and she caught her creation's gaze. But as if she had intended it when she had bestowed the curse, she was exempt, and her storm-grey eyes burned into the monster's red. The corner of her mouth quirked, languidly stretching, but in the echoed crack of a sob, she saw the blood-red of Medusa's eyes and how it seeped into worried hues across her eyelids and cheeks. An emotion too broken to fool anyone into thinking her dangerous.

Her grin faltered, her brow relaxed, and the goddess's stance melted into pity for the creature before her. Pity like she felt for mortals who were born too weak to survive winters. Pity that rolled through her like a disease when she heard the wails of wives and mothers in her temples as wars raged a half a world away. Pity that simmered in her stomach when her immortal siblings had their mortal lovers cast to the flames or the maws of beasts when her father's temper erupted.

What cowered before the goddess was not the monster she had expected – or hoped for – in the wake of tragic destruction her creation had left. Tears cascaded the scaled edges of Medusa's face, painting her in likeness to a child in costume.

'You are no more than a woman,' was all she said.

A shift, and Medusa's lip stopped trembling. Hands crumpled in the dirt fisted white-knuckled as she pushed herself up. Her shoulder blades pulled too, but as if she were a feral animal reanimated from the dead. At last, she stood before the goddess, the same height if her wrangle of snakes were considered. The image stole Athene's breath and thought.

'There is nothing less about being a woman,' Medusa murmured, lips split and moving wild to make her words clear. A thought flittered across Athene's mind; when was the last time Medusa had used her voice? The night she had begged for her life, or her death. The thought that Medusa's silence may have been bookended by her voice being thrown at Athene's ears each time struck her. Plenty of time to hone one's anger from unmitigated fury into a perfected barb. 'But why, *goddess*, do you perceive yourself as any different?'

Athene scoffed. 'I am far more than just a woman.'

'But you are a woman. A woman and a pawn to the machinations of men. When you fought over the golden apple to best other women, who would decide?' Athene declined to answer, for it was not even a god. It was a mortal boy. 'When Zeus grows aggravated by mortal disloyalty, it is you that is commanded to stifle them. Deign to support a mortal man in battle? He fails you and perishes. Or feigns cowardice to avoid honouring your gifts altogether.'

'You seem versed in the trials of my life,' Athene hummed, a pinch in her pursed lips.

'It was not the Fates' design that found me in your temple the night Poseidon followed, you know.'

Athene hummed. She had been told the story. All the gods hollered and cheered about it. 'It was your design to lure him in.'

'He raped me, Athene.' Medusa's voice echoed in the hollow of the forest. Goddesses do not feel the chill, but her skin rose. Her throat hammered with her pulse. 'I prayed to you and was loyal to your honour every day. But that man knew I would be there. I did not lure, and if you believe that, you are different to us.'

You are no different. She had assumed it was association with the gods, not other women.

'There is no blood or death that stains your skin, and yet you wear armour,' Medusa went on in her attacks. 'Who do you wear that aegis for, goddess?'

The only time Athene's fingers had been cold with grief, as she closed the eyes of her friend that Zeus had interfered with and gotten killed. He doubted his daughter, belittled this part of himself that was supposed to be the best of him. Despite his words of conceited praise, when it truly mattered that she proved him right, he proved her wrong.

A girl and a pawn to the machinations of men. Athene felt the tide of that grief burn up her throat to consume her again, as it had many years before and never again since. The day she stopped herself from being a girl and caring for them too.

The scene was still, serene. Only arrogance could protrude and seek to destroy it, and that was what Perseus did. Out of the corner of Athene's eye, more monster than man in the shadowy distance of her vision, the boy hunter appeared. He held the shield at the level of his eye, but as he peered over its crest every few stalking strides, she saw how ablaze his eyes were in the moonlight that had filled the forest. He sought to outwit, he sought to destroy, and he sought to take what no one was willing to give. Least of all, the mighty goddess herself.

Without thought, only the feathering of muscles in her jaw and fluttering of eyelids across tear-sheened eyes, Athene summoned her spear.

It was a fine piece of weaponry, taller than even she with a blade that glittered more in darkness than the Aegean did on the brightest of Apollo's days. A beat of satisfaction before she launched it through the air to strike the boy down. It impaled him and connected him to the earth in one resounding sound, echoed only in the vibrations it sent across the forest floor.

From his chest, darkness seeped, his eye's filled with glassy shock.

He, the son of king and princess, will be the one to lead the hunt and bear the fatal weapon.

Athene raised her brows. He certainly did bear the fatal weapon.

'It is bold to save me now when you could not fathom the concept before,' Medusa's voice scratched.

A statement enough to decimate a goddess, Athene moved forward, reaching to press her palm to the woman's chest. The hollow of the gorgon's neck settled like a cave against her skin as fingers wrapped the scale-skinned throat. Medusa sucked in a whisper of air, but with a soft caress of her thumb to the skin beneath it, Athene pulled the curse from the monster's marrow.

A reflection of the earth's own magic from the night she had bestowed the curse swelled around them. Breezes of summer danced through the snakes until they became dark ringlets of silken hair, light from a sun not present illuminated eyes from red to green, tusks to teeth, scales to skin.

'It is true, what I spoke that night,' Medusa's raspy voice whispered. 'You are no different.'

'I do so want to be different,' Athene protested. 'I want not to be like the gods.'

Medusa's brows knit together, and her shoulders slumped. 'You are not like them, Athene. The nature of your life dictates it in some respects, but you are like *us,* like women.' She dipped her head to catch the gaze of the goddess, to still with her ocean eyes the inner turmoil that was a tempest within the immortal's mind. 'You have suffered under the demands of man just as we have. Do you not see that you are callous as men are, that you are praised as cunning because it is what benefits them, that you are no more woman to them than I am guilty of the crime *they* said I was of?'

It stunned Athene for a moment, she was uncharacteristically speechless of witty retort or cutting comment.

'You *are* greater than us and could do more than to be their puppet, only sparingly granted the sun when they have been warmed enough.'

Epiphany dawned on her like it had not been cried to her the night of Medusa's cursing. 'I can save you.'

'To endeavour is to acknowledge our yearning for protection, and that is all we need,' Medusa said as she stepped closer, her hands rising to hold Athene's. Two hands as cold as the grave, two basking in eternal life, connected in trust.

The tug at her lips felt foreign in comparison to her usual grins, but she found that she could not help the smile that spread across her face in the safety of Medusa's presence and the kiss of moonlight. Yes, she would always be goddess, but it was her turn to worship. 'Protect them,' her lips murmured, the words a purpose she had found, never suspecting that she was searching. 'Save them, as I should have saved you.'

Medusa shook her head deftly with a coyness in her eyes. 'Save them, as you have finally saved me.'

...

Save them.

Athene erected a temple in her name atop the Acropolis, the greatest gorgonian present on her cuirass and never again amongst mortals.

Save them.

Medusa's tale, although butchered by man's tongue, has been soothed for millennia beneath the whispers of women.

Save them.

Embossed into coins and jewellery, inked between shoulder blades, gorgonians of new for protection of powerful women.

Save them.

Girls in their divine strength sport clothing that boasts *fuck the patriarchy* and Medusa's might.

Save them as you have saved me, and together we will save womankind.

ABOUT THE AUTHOR

HANNAH BISHOP

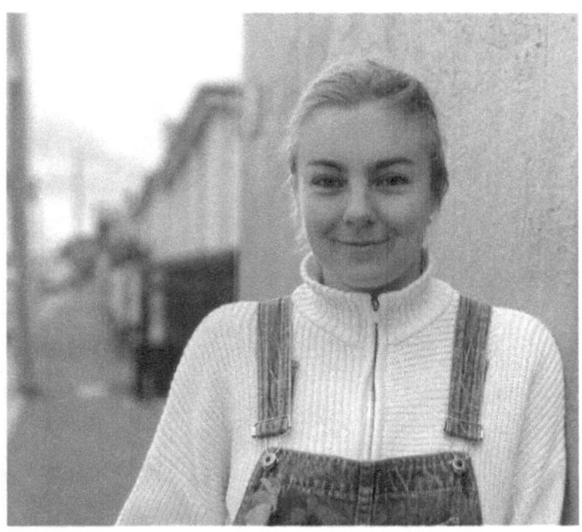

Hannah is a queer poet and fiction author with a degree in theatre studies and is undertaking a second degree in creative writing and publishing so that she may further her passions as a writer in the industry.

For as long as she could imagine, she has been daydreaming and writing, and when she's not doing that, she's got her head in a book or is fuelling her obsession with mythology and ancient history. Her favourite genres to read are fantasy and cosy crime but loves to read historical fiction when based upon a badass woman.

She hopes to one day write novels of various different genres, but for now is working on a fantasy series as well as a collection of short stories. A Queenslander by birth, she has found home in Tasmania with her fiancée, and furry children Scarlett the cat and Clover the rabbit.

hanrbishop.author

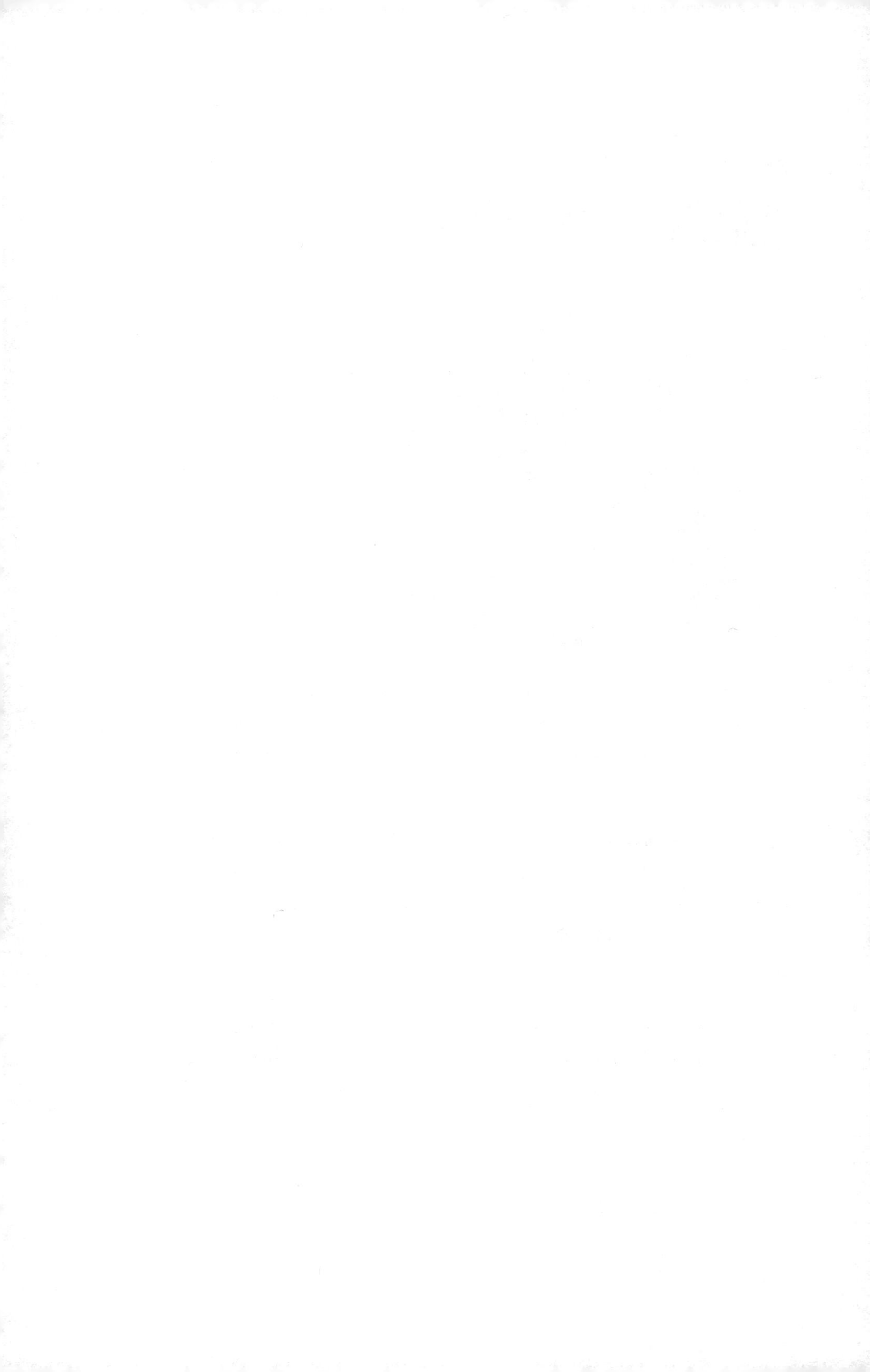

CHAPTER 7

YOU WERE ALWAYS THERE

Stacey Howes

Dedicated to my Mum,
Carmel Pompey.

You were always there. Every day of my thirty-nine years on this earth, my soul knew you were there. You were there for me before I needed you. You went before me to make sure I would be safe and loved. You paved a path for me as a child, teenager, adult, mother. And, I had no idea. No idea of the depth of your love. The sacrifices you willingly made to ensure I would be okay. The fierceness of your protection, always over me.

And when you left. When you took your very last breath – I felt it all vanish.

When I look back on our relationship, it wasn't always smooth. I grew up as a typical 'Daddy's girl' and flourished in his boundless love. I remember at a young age noticing you often appeared sad. I never knew or would have understood that your mum died a month after I was born, and that Dad had been my primary parent because of this. And maybe because of this, over time I became closer to Dad as a child.

But still, you were always there. I instinctively knew that. In my heart and in my soul, I knew I could always count on you.

In my mid-twenties, I remember the night I finally called to tell you about the abusive marriage I was in. You dropped everything. Drove through the night hours and hours to get to me and your grandchildren, then a newborn and a toddler. And in the preceding years, we lived close by, and you loved and guided us through the challenges on the other side of leaving an abusive relationship, teaching me how to advocate for myself and my children and being our strongest pillar, at every given moment.

And this was the beginning of our journey of love, healing and honesty. And for the following twelve years we grew closer and closer.

We knew you weren't well for some months, and we knew it was likely to be cancer. You had done all the right things, adjusted your diet, had countless doctor's visits and two biopsies. But I will never forget the day, the moment, when we were in your hospital doctor's office, and he said he was so sorry you had cancer, and it was terminal. The shock went through you, and you said that it can't be. You had things you wanted to do. The confusion and fear. Panic was over your face and in your voice. And the heartbreaking anguish I felt was that I could not fix anything. I could not alleviate it for you. I could not say anything that would make it better. At that moment, the world stopped. It stood still. I froze and watched in slow motion as the doctor asked if you'd been exposed to asbestos. I did not remember at the time, but the doctor said you had Mesothelioma Sarcomatoid cancer.

We thought you would get a diagnosis that could be treated. We expected it and planned to get some delicious takeout food for home afterwards. Only to buy the food and drive the thirty minutes home in disbelief and shock. I don't remember much of that evening except that once I went home later, and your grandchildren were in bed asleep, I sat in the dark, played a Fleetwood Mac CD and sipped wine. And then the deep agony that had been building inside me, burst. I have never felt so broken and afraid. I have never felt such sorrow and bewilderment and pain. I had never felt so vulnerable. Heaving sobbing. For my Mum, whose life is ending. Whose dreams were ending. Heaving sobbing. I was gripped by the overwhelming fear of not having you in my life and the realisation that you are my everything.

And then Fleetwood Mac's song 'Landslide' played. I cried harder as the foreseeing melodic words described with raw accuracy, my pain. But time makes you bolder. Even children get older. And I'm getting older too. I cried harder as the foreseeing melodic words played on and described with raw accuracy, my pain. At that point in my life, we had come through so much together and had built an incredible, mutually nurturing relationship where we loved and respected each other as the women we were. We were each other's cheerleaders and confidants, quick to help each other when needed and most of all, affirming and validating each other because we had both come to deeply trust one another. We both had gone through deeply painful trauma in our lives, we had become distrustful of many. We hid the deepest parts of ourselves, the most vulnerable parts that were the essence of who we were to protect our hearts from being destroyed again.

At that point, I had built my life around you. From the night you rescued your grandchildren and me, until now, we had all become gloriously entwined. It's like we had been given a beautiful chance to heal and create the relationship we always longed to have. We had our own routines of keeping in touch daily, regular dinners, sleepovers, holidays away, phone calls, texts, sharing social media memes and baking. Christmas and birthdays were always shared and indulged in. Over the years, we had some tough conversations about past and present hurts, with either one of us storming out of the house on more than one occasion. Over that time our love for each other made us work through things and heal as we both relaxed into our true selves and flourished into becoming best friends.

And your grandchildren. Your two darlings who you helped raise and who adored you. The fun sleepovers you would all have where you would feed them chocolate in the mornings, in bed! You were their world, too.

You didn't want a prognosis and over the last five months of your life, you fought hard to have as much time as possible with your beloved family and friends. And gradually the contents of the fridge and pantry became increasingly stocked with nourishing drinks, supplements and food to keep you feeling as well as possible and alive.

I wanted your remaining time on earth to be how you wanted it to be, no matter what. We made the most of each moment together, including all the time we spent in various hospital waiting rooms. As you slept more and more, those moments became more precious. While you slept during many of the car rides to your appointments, I would glance over at you as much as I safely could to deepen the memories of your presence in the front seat next to me. Because I knew that one day I would glance over, and you would not be there. Cuddled up on the front seat with a hot water bottle, blanket and a cushion to shield the tumour on your back. *My Mum.*

You spoke about how you didn't want to be a burden for me. I said that you were not a burden and by letting me take care of you was allowing me to love you in this way. And that you would do the same thing for me if it was reversed. It was never, ever a burden to look after you in your last months, Mum, it was an honour and a privilege that I will always cherish.

It was when you told me quietly one day, that you had the gurgle, that an alarming panic overcame me. I knew what you meant. Even though I knew you were dying, deep in my soul I feared the inevitable reality. And over the next few days, I operated in a state of deep focus, panic and disbelief, all at once. I slept in the room next to you, waking multiple times a night to listen for your breathing and woke up relieved you were still there. I knew what it meant when I could hear your loud, gurgled breathing. But it also meant you were still alive.

Each final moment that occurred since you told me about the gurgle, seemed to have sped up and I couldn't slow it down.

Recording your funeral wishes, a flurry of hospice nurses, a pain pump, ambulance to hospice. I stayed by your side as much as possible as your breathing became more laboured and drawn out.

When you took your very last breath and became still, it was like the window had slammed shut and your warmth was instantly gone.

Your guidance was gone.
Your direction was gone.
Your reassurance, gone.
Your love, gone.
Your hope, gone.

You were the sun and the moon to me, lighting the path and giving me direction. When you left, there was an instant blank. While you were still alive, even when you were barely alive, there was still a warmth on my skin and a fresh gentle breeze. When you took your last gasp of breath, everything was still. A void of not knowing what to do and not seeing a way forward replaced the sun and the gentle breeze. There was nothing.

And in the days and weeks that followed, I became completely undone. I did not know who I was, and the grief got deeper and deeper as I realised how much you really impacted my life. I felt fearfully exposed and vulnerable without your love, guidance and protection.

In every stage of my life, you were a compass to whom I looked to for direction. You were always 'home' to me, and I realised that you knew me far better than I thought you did.

You helped me and your grandchildren rebuild our lives and sprinkled your magic and sparkle of love and fun over us at any given moment. You supported me to gain multiple educational achievements and career opportunities which have profoundly shaped who I am today.

I took extended leave from work as I tried to fight my way through the darkest clouds of grief. I gave all of my energy to my children and in the times that I had to myself, I allowed myself to feel and contemplate the many emotions I was feeling, sadness, anger, shock, anxiety, loneliness. I began journaling again and with the help of my grief counsellor who I had been seeing since you were diagnosed, some close friends and family and some incredible books on grief, orphaned adults and the loss of a mother, I was able to understand grief a bit more and have my experience of becoming a motherless daughter and orphaned adult affirmed.

Around a year after you died, I joined a grief support group at the hospice, and I finally found a place where I could healthily express my pent-up grief-anger. It was deep and it was raging. And expressing it amongst those who were experiencing the same turmoil as me, was deeply healing. By the end of our sessions, my anger had mostly dissipated, and my mind was clearer.

What was surprising to me on this journey of healing, apart from the fact that I did not immediately realise that this was indeed the journey I was on, was how transformative the healing would be. It forced me to confront my deepest feelings, and I learnt that I had to truly sit with the pain I felt without any judgement or expectation of how I should respond. Old hurts surfaced; new hurts surfaced. I listened to each hurt and accepted them for what they were, I gained a new understanding and compassion for others and myself.

This led to me learning about boundaries which catapulted me into moving my family to a city where we could start fresh and create a life for the present. After you died Mum, many people told me to look for signs of you. I looked and I waited. Nothing. And then a few days before we moved, two praying mantises appeared at our back door. I was overwhelmed with awe and comfort, feeling strongly that these two fascinating insects represented my parents. I felt like they were there at a vital transition point in my life – supportive and assuring.

And after a long time of the deepest despair, depression and anxiety, I started to hear you. Your gentle warm voice, like the first feeling of warmth on the coldest, frostiest morning. The warmth you hope for in the cold and continuously look for glimpses of sunlight to peak out through the clouds or from behind the shadows.

Then you feel it. And it warms your skin, and it keeps warming you, and it gives you hope. It gives you relief. This is what it has been like for years after you died. I hear your guidance; I feel your warmth and I know it's you. It's like the warmest whisper of comfort and you are in my heart. 'Rest you say, don't forget to rest.' But mostly, I hear you say, 'Trust yourself. Stay connected to who you are and trust yourself.'

I hear your voice when I am taking time for myself and resting with a book in the sun. I feel your guidance when I have listened to my heart and not my head and have moved into a career and organisation that I am deeply connected to. I feel your hope when I am unsure and your voice inside me says to trust myself. I feel your protection when I realise how much you nurtured the special relationships in our lives and that these incredible people will always support me and look out for me.

I have learnt more about the struggles you went through, and I am in awe of the way you continued to try your best to look after your family while reconnecting with yourself. I can now look back and see and appreciate more of the struggles you endured because I have been in the midst of them in my own life too. I see the boundaries you had put in place to protect your energy and heart. You were determined to give hope to people and encouragement to never give up on themselves.

I wonder whether you prayed for us. I wonder whether you are paving the way. My new career pathway is in the very same sector that you worked in and in the very same building. I adore this career and as a precursor to you paving the way, I also partially worked in another building of the same organisation in another town, where you also worked for many years. And in each workplace, you are well known, respected and missed. And I feel so connected to you.

And over time, the sharpness of the grief I feel for you has softened somewhat. I am doing things I love, and my soul is joyous. My soul still searches for you. It longs for you. I don't think this will ever change. We are a part of each other beyond what we see on this earth. I have learnt to make room for the times when I have deep sadness and longing for you. I am amazed at the peace and strength you can get from honouring these feelings. It is not easy but there is a deep healing in honouring every true part of ourselves. Honouring the very essence of who we are and how we feel.

It will be five years since you passed Mum. It's gone fast, it's gone slow. I still instinctively pick up the phone to call you and tell you some news. I'm only just able to look at your recipe books and contemplate using them to feel connected to you. I'm only just able to open your beloved photo albums and linger over pages of love, history and connections just as you had done.

I realised that your love lives within me. It is in my heart from when you kissed my check and hugged me tight. It is in my heart from when I returned from holiday, and you lit the fire and had a hot dinner waiting. It is in my heart from when you told me how much you love me. It is in my heart from the many times we would laugh and talk for hours on end.

It's in my heart.

ABOUT THE AUTHOR

STACEY HOWES

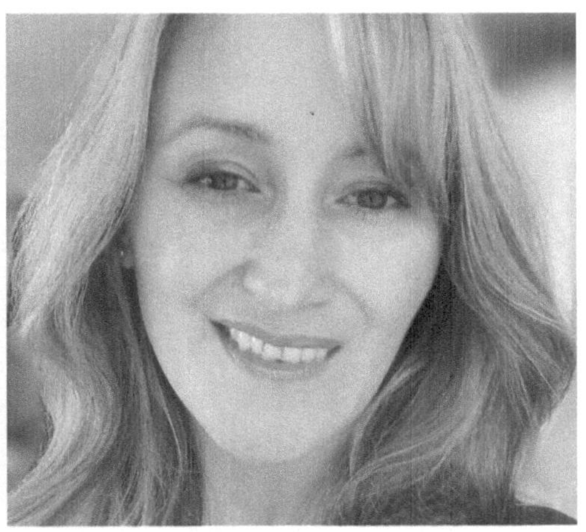

Kia ora, I'm Stacey. After my mother died a year before I turned 40, I began a profound and raw journey of becoming completely undone as an adult orphan. I experienced the deepest hurt and longing for a soul that seemed to no longer exist in this world. A soul that defined who I was as a person and directly influenced my everyday life without me being consciously aware of this. And throughout this tragedy, I made some surprising discoveries about love beyond death, seeing my mother as a 'whole human' and a deep desire to reconnect with the essence of who I am.

Part of the discoveries I made was the longing in my soul to write. Not to be extraordinary but to be real. I love deep and meaningful conversations of the soul because it is at this level of communication, where we truly connect as humans. And after many years of masking the longing to be authentically me, I am honouring this part of myself and all the 'flaws' of being an 'imperfect' human.

CHAPTER 8

THIS VERSION OF ME

Kellie Hannah

For Jessica, my watcher, my sister, my friend.
And to my husband Dave, for strapping in from start to finish,
'it'll be ok Deary me, it'll be ok'.

In this short Life
That only lasts an hour
How much – how little – is
Within our power.
—Emily Dickinson

My oldest son was waiting for me on the top step when I got home that day, he did not say anything, he just opened his arms and hugged me tightly. He did not let go, not until I was ready, his silent strength allowed me to take my first deep breath since hearing the news. *How is this even happening again?*

The diagnosis of breast cancer in my younger sister sent shockwaves through her life. In a moment, her world, and our collective worlds stopped. This feeling was familiar, it was too familiar. There was no preparation, even though my immediate family had done this cancer gig before, multiple times, it did not make it easier to understand or process. There were no answers, there was nothing that made any of it okay. She had already survived her first cancer, at the age of seventeen. *Why in the universe is this happening again?* Witnessing her move forward each day, all while navigating a new diagnosis, birthing her first child early to commence treatment, and then undergoing her double mastectomy left me, in total awe of her strength. My sister is a survivor. A true survivor! She has faced more in her thirty-three years than the average person. She has earnt that badge twice over. Cut from a strong cloth; just like our mother, and our mother is the strongest woman I know, a cancer warrior who lives with her diagnosis every day while still providing the most constant source of love, hope and strength.

My sister's breast cancer came with a surprise element, a hidden aspect, a life-changing and family-changing facet that provided the power of choice; without her experience, the gene mutation might have remained unknown, leaving myself and others in our family unaware of our risk until perhaps it was too late. The magnitude of this was not lost on me. How do you begin to thank someone for giving you a life-changing choice because they experienced a life-changing hell? The words thank you seem so minimal, they seemed selfish to say after watching her fight to survive. She had suffered so much, and I get to choose? Those two little words, in no way could ever capture the magnitude of what she experienced. Two little words that just did not in any way, seem enough.

What did it even mean to be a previvor?

It was being a pre survivor before the potential, more than likely event. It was about getting in first, taking control when risk was higher than not. And when you carry a positive BRCA1 mutation, for me, it was about doing everything possible to prevent an increased risk of breast and ovarian cancer. Having watched every female of my immediate family experience a cancer diagnosis, and then the treatment and recovery that follows, it was a life-changing choice. The journey of prevention is like a roller coaster ride. I was required to strap in and hang on tight, ready, or not, because the ride was set in motion. To clarify, I have never been a fan of roller coasters. This was not just a mere snap in of a seatbelt, and the coaster gently pulls away. It is an extensive journey of navigating emotions, choices, appointments, tests and scans. It is travelling hundreds of kilometres to and from each appointment, living rurally on the land equals no quick trip to anywhere. It is making decisions; many decisions and it consumes your life. Preparing myself with as much knowledge as I could, I moved forward each day, while always in the back of my mind the knowing of BRCA. It felt like a ticking clock, the alarm set, and you have no idea what time it is set for. It is a waiting, a constant state of oscillating between anxiety and empowerment, paralysis and progress. Some days, I rode the ride with my arms up high in the air feeling unstoppable. Other days, I was terrified and wanted to get off. Living with a constant whisper in my mind, a feeling of running, some kind of gauntlet. The knowing and the not knowing all rolled into one. It was during this preparation and planning time; I began to understand the gene's impact and its perpetuation within the family lineage. Genetics was something I had never thought about. Now it was something that consumed my life. I began to watch it reveal itself in the branches of our family tree, wrapping itself around more lives, with some of my cousins finding themselves on the same ride. They had entered the world of genetic mutations. It rippled out and would keep rippling out. It was a time, I began to fully comprehend the power of what my sister's hell had given me – what it had given to all of us, in our family tree – the privilege of choice. And I also recognised, just what my experience may give to others in my family, who might be watching.

I was fifteen the first time I learned that terrible things could happen to good people. Life can be short; it can change and spin off in any given direction and no-one knows what is coming next. My immediate family has had its fair share of trauma, illness, disease and death. I have watched. I have wondered, how so much can happen to one family. *Why them? Why not me?* Each time I would fill the useless feelings with an unconscious act of trying to hold it together. I have watched so many times, that I do not really know when anticipation took control of my life. The anticipation of what will be next, who will be next? I had lived with that for a lifetime! As the watcher, I learnt early that there is nothing that can be done, it cannot be changed. All that you can offer, is your thoughts, your presence, a silent promise that you will be there whenever you can. That you will wait with them. Hope with them. That you will witness and hold space. It was the watching and witnessing over so many years, which prepared me to make a choice. This was the reason that I could immediately see, such power in the now and why no matter how terrifying prevention looked there was no way, that I was just waiting and watching this gene do whatever it might do in my body. Not a chance. So, I strapped in!

When it came to speaking out loud, my intentions of having preventative surgeries, it not only informed my closest that I was going on this ride, but it also sent the intention out to the universe. A firm believer in the energy of the universe, constantly putting out what I choose and receiving what is needed. By saying my choice and intentions aloud, I could begin to own the decisions I had made. I received mixed reactions.

'Wow, that's a bit full on, isn't it?'

'Well, yes, I guess amputating your natural breasts and uterus is a bit full on. But hey, so is watching all the women in your family experience cancer and fight for their lives!'

'Well at least you get a boob job out of it!'

'A mastectomy is not a boob job!'

Or alternatively, the other reactions.

'Wow, you are so brave!'

'I can assure you; I am not brave, I'm just strapped in but thank you.'

'Please, tell your story, more people need to know you can make these choices.'

That is exactly what I plan on doing.

My surgery dates are anniversaries to me. They are etched in my life story. A birth, a death, a little of each. Not celebrated loudly, just quietly acknowledged when the dates roll around. Those dates celebrate the privilege of choice. My choice. The timing of my hysterectomy aligned with the greatest heartbreak I had ever experienced in life. The day of my father's funeral, I received a call with my surgery date, a week later I walked into the hospital a little messy and a little broken. My recovery was heavily clouded with saying goodbye to my dad, an exceptionally long goodbye with Alzheimer's Disease. The morning of my double mastectomy and reconstruction followed just over a year later. That morning, I walked into the hospital as ready as I could be, I had done a lot of work to prepare and this time I was not so broken and not so messy. Waking from my mastectomy surgery, the relief, the knowing that it was all done – all the choices, all the anticipation – done. My physical recovery from both of my surgeries was textbook, positive from start to finish. All pathology results clear. I didn't realise that once it felt safe, I would be exhausted. Not physically exhausted, but emotionally. Grateful and thankful for my results and yet completely detached from my body. I did not recognise the reflection staring back at me, scarred, numb and emotionally consumed with my unrealistic expectation of healing. I did not feel like any version of self I knew! I had assumed, that once the surgeries were done, the ride was over, and I could unstrap. I didn't realise the biggest loops were fast approaching.

'Ladies and Gentlemen, estrogen has left this building.'

Around we go, around we go and around we go again, this is menopause. It is the experience of dropping into every version of self and none, all of them, coming to surface, at any given moment. Unpredictable, regardless of it starting naturally, chemically or surgically. Each woman experiences it differently. We are all doing the best we can. Menopause is the time in a woman's life where we can suddenly feel the urge to express all forms of emotion and mostly in an unfiltered state. Introducing Patricia! My unfiltered menopausal alter ego. Not afraid to say what is on her mind – blunt, teary, unreasonable. Sleep deprived, brain fog, more blankets, turn up the air-conditioner, one leg out – literally a hot and cold being. My menopause is something I continue to work through, some days I feel like I am coming to the other side, others, I think, *Will this ever end.* The emotional turbulence that is menopause hits at any given time and space. Like grief, menopause rolls in and rolls out and can make you question everything, everyone, even yourself, more than you ever have before. I have found that there is connection in menopause, amongst your circle, all finding ourselves in a new part of life. All sharing our tips and insights with each other and feeling understood. Connection is vital, we are not alone in this club. I know that there will come a time that I reach the other side, as I have with so much of this experience. There are days I am proud of myself and can see the light and other days, well, there is always Metallica!

Ode to Metallica, providing a space of expression, that dates to a time in my teenage years, reminding me of when I spoke my truth loudly and boldly, without anticipation. Therapy for this menopausal woman, for the girl that wants to be heard, therapy for the grief and anger, released in raging lyrics – all without offending anyone.

Dear Metallica, do you realise that you have generations of menopausal women who have always loved you, blasting your music out to the universe?

Metallica, I know that they are not for everyone, but here sits what was once a teenage girl who belted out their lyrics loudly, as my therapy for release on those harder days. And now they are the therapy for Patricia!

No kind of healing begins without the unpacking. The unpacking of the experience, the changes, the transition. The unpacking of self. Now, I love nothing more than a good cleanse, to unpack and throw away what no longer fits, what no longer works. When it comes to my house, my stuff, I do it openly and happily give things away. When it comes to myself, I prefer to do this privately. My unpacking requires time to digest. I cocoon. Cocooning is my go-to. It is my innate response to processing anything. It is necessary. It is a time full of thoughts and feelings, most of which I keep to myself. However, this time, this cocooning was not quiet. It was consuming. There was no grace or understanding within, at least not for myself. I felt I had failed. My complete detached, unfiltered, numb, self, just throwing my thoughts out there, reasonable, or not. A time filled with internal self-doubt, harsh self-reflection, and unachievable expectations of what my healing should look like. A time where I encountered loss of important relationships and loss of myself. I could not give to anyone when my cup was empty and my expectation of myself was high and hard. It was a time I was extremely fortunate to have my husband's strength to lean on. He is not a loud or boastful man. He is quiet and steady. He is patient and practical. He has held my hand, stood by me, stood up for me and accepted every one of my choices. He lets me breathe, heal, grieve, cocoon, and knows when I need my sisterhood.

The power of sisterhood. Women, related by blood or choice in shared experiences are a force to be reckoned. My male-dominated world, I would not change with my three sons and my husband, the love in my life, however my estrogen negative household is also why I value and nurture my female relationships as best I can. A sisterhood that has shared much laughter, tears and memories. These women are the holders of my deepest secrets and mirrors of my true self. They are my ride and dies. The ones who understand my silence, as profoundly as my words. They know my ways, they celebrate my achievements and navigate through my adversities, alongside me. It can be the quiet conversations over tea, the wild laughter that fills the room, this sisterhood, are the unconditional shoulders I leaned on. Surrounding me, each in their own way, they could see past the broken and showed me that I had not failed. They remind me that imperfection is a universal experience and is in no way, a reflection of our worth. They embrace each version of me without judgement, without condition and with love. They are my watchers, with no expectation, and they held sacred space when I needed it the most.

It has been almost six years since I learnt of my BRCA1 mutation. Five and four years respectively since my surgeries and walking out as a previvor. What started as a transition for my body, continues to transition my life. There are days I look back and honestly cannot believe I am here. From a time that felt so full of anticipation, frozen in what was next to come, and I find myself here recognising that each version of me has evolved to the next. I am not finished, there are still things I try to make fit; not even recognising it, until it shows up. The difference is now when it does show up, I can release the feelings of anticipation. I can release, the expectations and the waiting. This version of me knows how to put things down a little better. She has learned to trust in the process of life, trust the timing, and trust in the power of living in the now and not in anticipation of the future. She knows, to evolve requires healing and healing is not one specific fix. It is moving through the triggers, through the trauma, through the conditioning. Healing is about waking up and living. It is continuous and it is lifelong. Healing is about being whatever version is needed now.

She sat with me that day and let me cry. She did not say it will be okay; she did not try to fix it, she just let me cry. The emotion, a defeated, forty-nine-year-old, blubbering mess. My tough exterior broken in the honesty of the authentic understanding and the release of any expectation. She has always been able to see through the layers, through the filters I put up, never have I been able to hide anything from her. As her older sister, I have tried, but she is connected, intuitively to me and so she knows.

She was watching. She knows better than anyone, the experience of moving forward, while still letting go. She knows better than anyone how to not let the anticipation steal away the joys of life. She shows me that everything we go through in our lives does not continuously need to be carried with us. She shows me how to put it down.

That was the day, my sister reminded me, life must be lived, every day, not in your fear but in your truth. And she continues to show me that authenticity and living in the now, will always trump anticipation, and it is in the letting go, that you will find your version of self.

And again, those two little words.

So minimal in their sound, so massive in their sentiment.

Thank you, sister, thank you.

ABOUT THE AUTHOR

KELLIE HANNAH

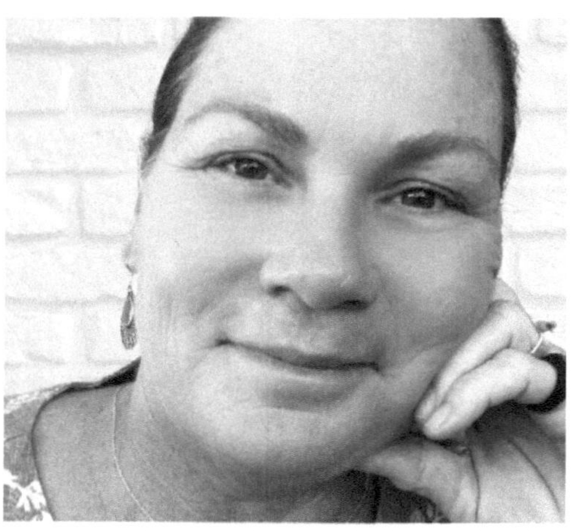

Kellie Hannah lives her life on the land, alongside her husband on their third-generation farming property, near the small rural town of Westmar in Western Queensland. Raising sons that are now adults and working as a teacher's aide for the past 14 years, Kellie has dedicated herself to education, nurturing young minds within her community. Creatively inclined, Kellie uses various forms of expression, a lover of writing, graphic design, videography, photography and also creating her small batch candles. She is passionate about capturing moments in time, often recording them in either words or pictures and she loves to explore new ideas and mediums of expression. Now in a stage of life filled with freedom, Kellie is embracing new positive opportunities, simple country living, frequent trips to the ocean and the love of her family and friends – the important things in life.

kmhannah.journal

CHAPTER 9

I AM MORE THAN ME, I AM MY COMMUNITY

Gina Kasmas

This story is dedicated to my mother Ekaterina Kasmas,
who did her best to hold on to her feminine power in a man's world.
Her story continues with me. Thank you, Mum,
for showing me what it is to always keep going.

Belonging. I've never really known what this feels like, consistently. But I have known belonging for moments. These moments are the reason I never stopped seeking my way back. When I knew belonging, it warmed the cockles of my heart and seeped through my entire being encircling my cells with emotional safety. It solidified my belief and trust in my life, and in humanity.

I wanted to feel this way all the time, to know I belonged. To be accepted for the way I saw the world. For the way I thought, the way I looked. Isn't belonging what every mother wants for their child in the schoolyard, and what every adult longs for?

After decades of searching, looking under many rocks and getting lost in rabbit warrens, I realised that feeling like I belong was as much a fundamental human need as food, water and shelter.

Watching the women in my life growing up, I observed the power they had to decide who belonged and who didn't. And they used this power for their own reasons, often with collateral damage.

Women know how important it is to feel that we belong, because we're biologically wired to grow and support life. Belonging keeps us connected to life, so that we may thrive. Without belonging, we might survive, but we don't thrive. Thriving doesn't happen in isolation, not for humans anyway.

We're not meant to be lonely. We need others for touch, affection and protection, so that we may thrive. The warmth of another human body can be healing. Loving and caring companionship is life-affirming and can make the difference between a person being emotionally stable, or mentally unwell.

We're nourished when we allow ourselves to trust another, and when this other holds us safe as we trust them with our sharing.

We know that empathy, compassion and kindness are nutrition for life. As women, we're privileged to birth new life if we choose to, the knowledge of this sacred life-giving miracle existing in the deepest stratum of our being. Whether we have children or not, we're intimately aware of the natural urge to propagate life through everything that pulses.

Why then, do women display life-denying behaviours, enacting quiet and underhanded acts of violence to each other? Why do women decide they don't like someone, and then collude with others to exclude them? Why do other women join in this collusion, when they have no personal issue with the person being excluded? Why do women compete with women to bring each other down, instead of collaborating which brings the other up, every time?

For the good of the whole or just some who want to rule?

Naturally we flock to those we have something in common with. Academics like to discuss their current research and evolving concepts. Business people discuss growth ideas to stay buoyant. Law enforcers have rules to keep them safe on the streets. Mums spend time in mothers' groups with newborns. Like-minded people help us share both the joy and challenge of a common purpose so that we may learn and grow together, so that we may experience the breadth of emotions that make us human and still know we are normal.

Exclusion that damages isn't about common interests but denying a person their rightful sense to belong, based on the opinion of one or two others.

If you're excluded, you feel you don't belong. If you exclude someone, you affirm your own sense of belonging. The two are opposites yet the same. They're about survival and safety and neither action supports the whole to thrive.

Women who have the power to exclude and cast out another because they don't like them, are concerned about their survival just as much as the person they are casting out. Will they measure up to the woman who succeeds in this world? 'Will I be smart enough, strong enough, attractive enough, to find the right man or woman, the right friends, the right employer, the right connections, so that this world I live in will accept me? So that I will survive? So that I won't be abandoned to the wayside, for the vultures to come and pick me to death?'

Because we've all seen that person who was left by the wayside, forgotten, abandoned. And we will do anything in our power to ensure we won't ever find ourselves there, if we can help it.

If you've experienced exclusion and bullying, yes it may be easier to go it alone in life, telling yourself you don't need anyone. But this will only lead you down a one-way road to a lonely dead end. Without connection to others, we feel like a pimple on the arse of the universe. Lost, like a leaf being blown this way and that. Connection to others anchors us on this great matrix of life, keeping us from falling over the edge, or getting caught up by gusts of wind and into black space.

You may see yourself through the eyes of the people in these stories, whichever side of the grievous end of exclusion you may have been on.

Sarah, 5 – was a delicate-looking and sensitive young girl. She had a problem at school, she kept peeing herself in public. No one wanted to be her friend. She spent every day by herself. As small children, we were terrified when we saw her face crumble and tears flow as her body involuntarily released yet another puddle of pee. Sarah was abandoned to the wayside. Eventually she left the school and there was no explanation of what had happened. At five years of age, we learned that being left to the wayside meant abandonment, and we decided we would do anything in our power to make sure this would never happen to us.

Sylvia, 16 – despised her twelve-year-old cousin, Teresa, simply because Teresa was taller, and growing into a willowy young teenager. Sylvia knew she would never be as tall, or as graceful, even though she was beautiful in her petite stature. She bullied Teresa when the parents were out of earshot repeatedly telling her how unattractive she was, how big her stature was, how clumsy and unappealing she looked. Teresa grew during these sensitive identity-forming years believing she was not only unattractive, but unworthy of love.

Barbara, 36 – was evicted from her women's spiritual development group because the leader of the group, Kate, decided Barbara had not evolved enough. Barbara was simply there for companionship with like-minded people and shared learning. She looked forward to their weekly catch ups and loved the support of the group. Barbara was also attracting new clients as a therapist and growing her business. Kate felt threatened. She told Barbara that her energy was not right for the group. A devastated Barbara threw in the towel and stopped providing therapy sessions to people who needed it, and it would be one year before she picked it up again.

Julie, 45 – had been trying to have a baby for ten years. Her social circle and friends were married with kids. Julie and her partner noticed they were being invited to social functions less and less. The women in the social group decided that because Julie and her partner didn't have children, they weren't the right fit for their social circles. But no one asked Julie, who wanted their companionship, they were her friends, her people. This careless and thoughtless exclusion was the tipping point for Julie. She consequently left her relationship, resigned from her job, and abandoned everything she once enjoyed. For two years she grieved, while she emotionally and mentally built herself up again to step out into the world.

Bridget, 52 – was simple, kind, with no airs and graces. The other women in her group would meet for coffee after class but wouldn't invite Bridget. She didn't dress like they liked to dress, and she didn't speak like they did. Even though Bridget felt the heart-squeezing painful pinch of exclusion, she didn't give up on these women because she wanted companionship. They finally invited her to coffee, and she was thrilled. They told her they'd be back at the same coffee shop next week, at the same time. The following week she turned up to the coffee shop again, but they weren't there. They'd changed the location, but no one told Bridget. Bridget was devastated.

These events forced people to sink or swim. They sunk at first, and eventually learned to swim in new streams.

Maybe these experiences made them clearer and stronger versions of themselves, maybe they forged their characters. But at what cost? Are they necessary experiences? Do we need to be subjected to cruel and thoughtless behaviours, acts of emotional violence, bullying and exclusion, just to become a more evolved and better version of our self? Not everyone is a warrior. Not everyone bounces back.

Well-meaning people have all sorts of advice.

You don't need people like that in your life.

Find your own tribe of people to connect with.

Better off alone than with people like that.

They don't deserve you.

You need to learn to enjoy your own company.

And finally, 'What doesn't kill you will make you stronger.'

What doesn't kill us *won't* make us stronger, it will make us weaker, until we find the right support to help us heal. For some of us, this can take many years.

What will you do next time?

Just a few kind words spoken, a listening ear, or a thoughtful gesture, opens the space to inclusion and belonging, to create a more emotionally and mentally healthy community.

We all belong in the groups we choose to participate in and contribute to. The small clique can risk the wellbeing of the larger community. Is it worth risking the whole to resolve a desperate need to survive?

We, as women, have the power to choose differently, every day.

Will you do it differently next time?

Will you allow your natural life-affirming qualities to lead the way, instead of your life-denying dark side to rule?

Will you use your power wisely next time and invite the outlier to be in your group?

Will you see the whole rather than just your small part in it?

Will you stop from getting caught up in pack mentality to exclude another just so you can fit in?

Will you accept the diversity of individuals to create a healthier community?

Will you care enough about our collective capacity to love each other more, to include another rather than exclude them?

If you do exclude someone just because you can, will you be willing to accept the consequences of your actions and the ripple effect of pain that you cause another? Will you stop and think about why you're excluding them, and question whether you are competing with them because of an irrational fear that you may be the one left by the wayside, and you will do anything to make sure it's them, and not you?

And will you forgive yourself, knowing you've been bred to survive and compete for a perceived and mistaken scarcity of love and companionship, and commit to making a different choice next time?

And if you are the one who has been excluded, will you have enough faith in humanity not to give up, but to persevere in connecting with others? Will you give yourself permission to keep trying, knowing that there is nothing wrong with you, that you're just a person who wants to feel you belong?

A sense of belonging is the compass that helps us find the way back home when we feel lost.

Belonging is essential to our health and wellbeing. We are more than just us. We are an inextricable part of the communities we live in. We matter because we are here, present and alive.

Remember that as you keep travelling through this mystery of living.

'I am more than me, I am my community.'

ABOUT THE AUTHOR

GINA KASMAS

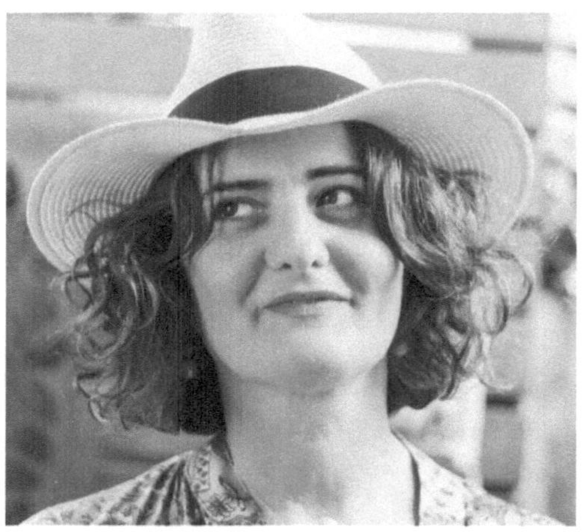

Yiasou! I came to writing later in life and I'm grateful to have found a channel for my analytical mind. I do my best to write openly about the struggle that is inherently human, doing life the best way we can, and recovering from emotional pain when life doesn't always go to plan. Trauma can leave invisible wounds that take longer to heal than we expect, and I have recovered from my own, and they took longer than I thought. As the old saying goes, time heals all wounds. By bringing people's stories to life and reflecting on what might have been, I hope my words will guide others toward grace, peace and acceptance, the place from which better life outcomes can emerge.

ginakasmas

www.ginakasmas.com

CHAPTER 10

HAPPINESS AND METAMORPHOSIS

S. A. Sisika

To my beautiful friend Beth,
you looked at this chapter with both your artistic experience and your perspective as a person that knows me inside and out. Thank you for consistently holding my heart in your hands and keeping it safe.

At the strange, transitory age of twenty-seven, I've been pondering happiness. *What does it mean for me, and what does it look like?* I've been thinking about who I used to be, and the space between me and her. How different her wants were. Who she thought she was, versus who I am. She was constantly on a rollercoaster of emotion and a happy person was not something she thought herself to be. She had dreams of moving to London and being the single rich aunt who travelled the world and had so many stories of her adventures, constantly moving was the only way to be. Her deeply ingrained religious beliefs and absolute view of the world were her compass and she was constantly playing judge and jury. Her self-talk of *Perfection is all there* *is so try harder,* got her to where she wanted to go, but the end result never felt good enough. The goal posts kept moving, the praise always felt hollow. She moved through the public world as an insecure person who wore a mask of confidence and moved in the privacy of her own home as a highly sensitive and angry child, lonely in a family of five, emoting at the world.

Could she have ever seen the path that I eventually took her on? I'm still dragging her, kicking and screaming. Out of all the wishes she had for herself to be an independent girl boss trailblazing across Europe, I wonder if she could have ever predicted that I would take her on a journey back to herself. She was tough and had it all figured out, self-aware, hyper independent and intellectual. *What else would she possibly need to learn about herself?*

We were the first born raised by a family of firstborns – our mother, our father, and our mother's parents, who we mostly grew up around. There's a strange emotional unavailability you find in firstborns, maybe it's the crushing weight of expectations, responsibility, or parents who relied on us to hold down the fort. Maybe it's the pressure to be everything our parents couldn't be. Or to be everything they wanted for us with the pressure to prove ourselves to everyone around us. We constantly felt like our family's pride and at the same time its biggest disappointment. Love felt like it cost something, and unconditional softness was something foreign to us. We were the ones who saw our parents figure out that they were responsible for life, we had to watch our parents grow up, quickly. We knew our parent's secrets. They trusted us with things that children probably shouldn't know, and we saw things the younger ones didn't. We were clued in like no one else in the family because knowing things kept us safe.

Firstborns tend to leave the nest earlier to spread our wings and realise our adult lives, missing out on a lot of our siblings' milestones. The disconnect that is created in firstborns from our siblings has always been intriguing. Even now in my late twenties, I'm learning about the things I missed out on, and the feeling of isolation hits the same way.

Her mother moved out at the age of eighteen, around the same age, her father was shipped off to the Army. Her grandmother to university. Her grandfather to the Navy. All of them leaving their siblings behind. Her life was governed by the whim of where the military needed her father, her grandfather, and their fathers. Be it war, or the other side of the country, two thousand kilometres from that friend that she just got to know and had felt like she really belonged. She needed to be adaptable, she had to start over in a new city, a new school, a new neighbourhood – every two years. By the age of twelve, she perfected being a chameleon. At eighteen, she'd had to start over more times than someone double her age and life experience had, she felt helpless and out of control in all of it. Her identity was an amalgamation of her parents, sisters, friends and whatever new city she was in. But it shattered to pieces when she was on her own. Worse, when someone asked her about who she was, or what she thought about the world. God forbid, someone ask her about something more than the weather, someone disagree or ask her why she thinks what she does. If she wasn't right, if no-one agreed with her, if no-one validated her, she would curl in on herself and want to fade into the background. Yet, she was headstrong, stubborn. The world was black and white. Shades of grey were not possible, they were not okay, they were not... right.

There was no room for nuance and complexity and changing your mind. There was her way or the highway and guess what? Her highway was actually the only way. She didn't get it, but I do. I see how she was moulded into a person who was able to turn herself into whatever someone wanted her to be, or whatever she felt like the situation demanded of her, a walking contradiction since she violently demanded others to be who she wanted.

You can only imagine the social survival skills she picked up along the way. She knew how to make friends quickly, connect with someone over the smallest of things, she was a party girl who was up for almost anything. She was quick witted, funny, reading the room with ease and picked out the most flexible, easy-going people. The trickiest skill, the one that has its claws lodged into me to this day, its roots so deeply embedded in me, is that she was so incredibly talented so as to put herself in situations where someone *needed* her. A survival instinct telling her to build her community, by any means necessary, and her inner older sibling asking, 'Who will let me take care of them?'

Looking at her now, I see she wanted so badly to be chosen, to not be abandoned, she needed to be needed. She wanted someone to tell her they'd always need her around, that she'd be the first pick for a shoulder to cry on, or moving house, or a weekend trip away. Maybe she couldn't admit it to herself, but she always needed everyone, she sacrificed parts of herself for the people around her in the hopes they would do the same when she came calling. I've come to realise this is something we might always share and that our happiness has been, and might always be, connected to being needed for a sense of purpose. I used to see this with shame but understand it as the way she and I view our completely natural desire to feel loved, to find our people, the ones that want us around without having to be begged. She put herself in so many situations she didn't want to be in. She went to parties when her body told her to stay at home. She hung around people who wouldn't care if she dropped off the face of the earth, but she still fought so hard for them to like her. *My God, all she wanted was to be liked.*

What if they fall in love with me?
What if I become their best friend?
What if this is my new community?

Happiness was dependent on another, always. She was always chasing that dopamine hit. Determined by her mother's mood, or how many friends texted her that day, whether she got invited to that party or not, if her crush liked her back, if she felt loved and included by her sisters. Happiness was dependent on how she thought other people saw her, or whether she thought she was good enough. Because of this, happiness has been an abstract and elusive construct up until very recently.

Despite unlearning the dependence on my external world for happiness, on being chosen for a sense of purpose, it is still what love feels like to me. Being chosen over and over without having to earn it. Yet, I still get it, this nagging desire to be the best friend, the favourite daughter, the favourite sister or cousin. It was, and still is exhausting. I wish I could go back and shake her and yell, 'Aren't you tired?'

That adaptable girl with a hard exterior, just wanted someone to hold her long enough to get to her gooey, soft centre. I wish I could go back, hug her, and tell her, 'I know you're tired.' Amongst all the habits I've shed in the last couple of years, I have to fight this way of thinking every day. It's a hard-wired belief in me, deep down, a written code that says, *If you don't do this, you'll end up alone.*

If you asked me, when or how she became me, I couldn't put my finger on an event or a point in time. At some point in my therapy journey I had to become open to completely filleting myself for a stranger, and then even more painfully, I had to admit that, in many aspects, I was responsible for a lot of my unhappiness.

In no way was it easy. Flash forward to today, and I've realised some days I *still* don't think I'm good enough. I've had to confront myself on things I didn't even know I believed about whether I was pretty enough, or smart enough, or cool enough, or funny enough. I've had to practise looking at the facts of situations that take me back to my old self, to give myself space and watch that old thinking pass me by, to be present instead of in the past, to hone my problem solving, and to treat the adults around me as, well, adults, who have their own thoughts and beliefs, none of which being my business.

I've also learned that I am nuanced and complex, and

so was my past self, and so is everyone around me. We are all many things at once and just trying to do our best. What I've learned, particularly about happiness, is that it also goes hand-in-hand with forgiveness, and I'm constantly having to forgive myself. Forgive myself for the things I did years ago when I felt hopeless and out of control, for the things I did last week, when I was lonely and wanted the sweet, exciting taste of chaos. I've forgiven myself for the person I was because she didn't know any better and didn't have the tools that I can proudly say I have today.

So, after all of this learning and forgiveness... *Am I happy?*

I think I'm finally okay with myself and with not being chosen. I'm at peace with the knowledge that I'm not for everyone and an empowering thought is that not everyone is for me. I'm finally content with my own company and I can choose who is in it. I have come to terms with where my life is at and I'm not forcing it to be something else, not forcing myself to be someone else. I have found my people and they love me for the dork that I am. I'm starting to truly trust my instincts for the first time in my life and I'm recognising people and spaces that make me act like someone I'm not.

I'm recognising what it feels like to know my worth and I think I'm a little jealous of people who've always known. I'm realising happiness is a way of being and moving through the world rather than an end goal. It's letting go of the things I can't control and being grateful for the things that I can. It's allowing myself to experience peace over survival instincts and giving myself the time and space to process my thoughts and emotions. It's choosing to be present and not fighting to make my reality fit expectations in my head. In a way, this makes happiness something that is all around me, a collection of choices that I can grasp at, at every second, every minute of the day if I so choose.

Am I happy? I am trying to be a person that has the skills and opportunity to be.

ABOUT THE AUTHOR

S. A. SISIKA

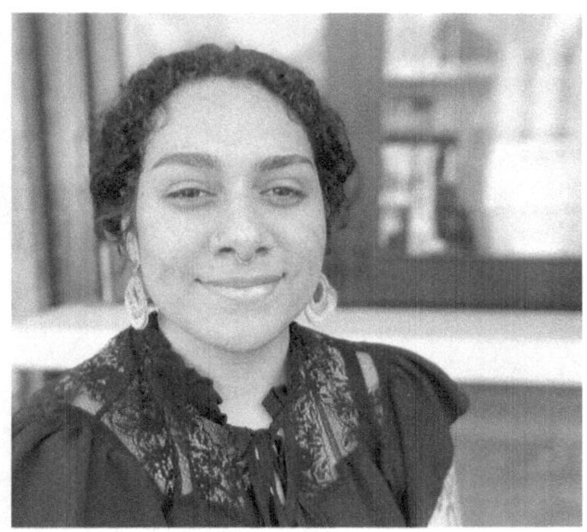

S. A. Sisika is an emerging Papuan-Australian poetry and novel writer based in Canberra. Her educational background is in Psychology, Indigenous Studies, and Music Performance. Moving From Papua New Guinea to Australia with her family when she was eight years old, Sisika continued to move around Australia every two years for her father's work, at a young age she embraced music, poetry and storytelling to express herself in times of uncertainty, fear, and sadness. This love of music and writing only became stronger throughout highschool and university, where words became a powerful tool to help navigate life's ups and downs. Through her writing, S. A. Sisika aims to tap into emotions which lurk under the surface, waiting to be spoken to. Her writing explores love, friendship, relationships, self-discovery, identity, and emotional truths. She enjoys writing about personal reflections, the good, the bad, and the ugly, the what ifs, and could have beens. She hopes to empower readers to explore the deepest parts of themselves and to express their inner worlds.

tealeavesandbiblichor

CHAPTER 11

HOLDING SPACE FOR OURSELVES AS WE NAVIGATE THE SPACES IN BETWEEN

Jessica Savage

For Cam and Harry.
I will love you (exactly as you are),
forever and always.

WHAT DOES IT MEAN TO HOLD SPACE?

Holding space is the act of being deeply present with someone. It requires the ability to be or become an empty vessel, which by default enables us to 'hold space.'

- It means allowing what is, to be.
- It means adopting a beginner's mindset. This asks us to show up as a beginner, complete with the openness and eagerness that comes naturally to those approaching something brand new.
- It means actively listening.

- It means walking the road alongside someone.
- It means not offering unsolicited advice, suggestions or comments.
- It means an intentional awareness of our own privilege. Among other things, this influences our bias and prejudice (which is why it is mentioned here). We must remember that we don't know what we don't know and so, it is imperative that we actively seek to develop our knowledge and understanding of what this might be.
- It means showing up without attachment, expectation or judgment.
- It means being brave.
- It means embodying love, kindness, compassion and acceptance.
- And, last, but not least – it means the person across from you is left feeling wholeheartedly seen, heard, held and received, exactly as they are, right now.

Now... I invite you to read the above, with yourself in mind. It is important to remember that we are talking about holding space for ourselves, not others, here.

WHAT ARE SPACES IN BETWEEN?

I have become intimately accustomed with in between spaces in my life. They often feel like being in some kind of limbo land.

In between spaces are...
The pause that unites an inhale, with an exhale.
The natural contraction that occurs before expansion...
... what often feels like, the messy middle.

Otherwise known as liminal space, they are voids of empty space – something preceding and something following. When we transition from one place, state or experience to another, usually while change is occurring, or brewing at the very least, we land in this space: the in between space.

WHAT TYPES OF TRANSITIONS LEAD US TO LAND HERE?

There are endless examples of the varied transitions we come across in life, some less complex and complicated than others!

They might look like:
the flicker of a spark,
a dream or desire you desperately feel called to bring to life.

They might look like:
grief and/or loss, in any way, shape or form.

They might look like:
adverse health challenges that possess the potential to curtail our capacity, alter our ability and/or involve our identity.

They might look like:
relationship milestones or shifts in relationship dynamics.

They might look like:
conception, pregnancy, labour, the birth of a baby *and* the postpartum period.

They might look like:
the start of something new, a job, business, income ceiling and/or location.

WHAT WILL WE DISCOVER IN THESE SPACES?

There lies within so many of us, an innate desire to influence the outcome of a situation. Although we are never truly in control of anything; control is purely an illusion. This is why – as humans living a human experience – detaching from a particular outcome isn't always easy. It can feel challenging for us to actually allow that resistance to be released.

Liminal space can be activating as it asks us to hold a mirror up in front of ourselves and see what we may not want to see, firsthand. This type of space encourages us to step up and rise into a higher version of ourselves, our future selves. It asks us to consider the work we are required to do... and, if we are honest with ourselves, truly *need* to do, in order to show up as the best version of each of us.

So how do we not react in a way that is detrimental to us, when we don't have a handle on that outcome, or perhaps even have a sense that the outcome we will receive is not the one we want for ourselves? How do we respond to the impatience and frustration – and all other relevant emotions – that are likely to arise when resistance and our ego start to set in?

There are an array of feelings likely to arise *in* in between spaces: stress, impatience, vulnerability, trust to name a few. If and how we choose to allow and move through these – physically, mentally and emotionally – contributes significantly to our overall experience of being in an in between space. We may require support from a professional with this. This decision requires discernment, as we are all unique, one-of-a-kind beings and each and every one of us needs to be considered with care on a case-by-case basis.

It is important to recognise here that our emotions are the drive behind our behaviour. In addition to this, our individual mental state and level of emotional sensitivity affect how we respond to our own feelings and the world around us. That said, the closest we can actually get to being in control and asserting any influence in situations we don't have control over, is self-awareness and self-regulation of our own feelings.

HOW CAN WE ENSURE WE ARE HOLDING QUALITY SPACE FOR OURSELVES?

We can do this by making ourselves a priority. It is important that our essential needs are met. Self-care is imperative and integral in being able to hold space for ourselves, in a way that genuinely serves us, sustainably. We must treat ourselves with the same respect we so generously bestow upon others and let go of any expectations we have placed on ourselves.

We can do this by slowing down, quietening our ego and tuning in to our intuition.

We can do this by cultivating deep self-trust. Deepening our own sense of self-trust will steady us through any self-doubt that may arise. We can be our own North Star, always.

We can do this by taking one step at a time.

We can do this by doing whatever best supports our nervous systems to both be and stay grounded. This will look different for each of us.

We can do this by allowing ourselves to feel whatever it is that we are feeling; without judgment. Permitting our emotions to rise and fall on their own timelines, just like waves ebb and flow in the same way. Simply noticing them as they come and go. May we also trust our need to receive external support with the process, if this comes up for us.

We can do this by tending to the thing we don't want to tend to!

We can do this by unshackling from what is known, to make way for what is unknown.

We can do this by releasing fear of judgment, especially in

relation to the way in which do or don't show up.

We can do this by detaching from the expectations and projections of others, that are not ours to meet or carry in the first place, unless we choose to.

We can do this by consciously choosing to break free from enmeshment.

We can do this by communicating and honouring our own boundaries, with discernment. These are terrific tools in managing our time, energy and resources. It is relevant to note here that we must also keep coming back to fine-tune our discernment. Life is ever evolving and so, it makes sense that this does not remain static as it will shift and change over time, and with different experiences too.

We can do this by nurturing a deliberate and devoted relationship with patience.

We can do this through circular leadership – no pedestals, no hierarchy, no-one to please and no-thing to prove.

We can do this by radically accepting *all* of who we are.

We can do this by remembering how powerful we *already* are.

ENCOURAGING AFFIRMATIONS FOR ALONG THE WAY

I allow myself to be.
I am worthy exactly as I am.
I shed old and outdated stories.
I find peace in letting go.
I am deserving of rest.
I accept that not everything is perfect, and that is ok.
I choose to focus on what I can do.
I remain connected to my vision.
I act as though I have already arrived on the other side of this space.

GUIDING OURSELVES TOWARDS THE 'GLIMMERS'

Whereas 'triggers' are known to dysregulate our nervous systems, 'glimmers', a term coined by Deb Dana that describes delightful moments discovered in the details of our day-to-day, can be spectacularly supportive in regulating our nervous systems.

To illustrate, here are a few examples:

Micro-moments in Spring: Noticing newborn lambs in the paddocks. Discovering daffodils in the garden. Encountering more daylight, with which to play.

Micro-moments in Summer: Feeling sand between your toes, as you walk barefoot on the beach. Witnessing sunlight filter through the leaves of a tree. Sensing the warmth of the sun on your face.

Micro-moments in Autumn: Falling leaves. The chemistry of colours that surround you. Splashing in puddles, spontaneously!

Micro-moments in Winter: Cosying up on the couch, next to a roaring fire. Standing still outside, as the snow swirls around you. Listening to the sound of rain on the windows, whilst snug as can be (under layer upon layer of blankets) in bed.

Practicing gratitude for what already exists in our immediate reality is an excellent way to ensure we remain present. This involves taking the time to acknowledge what you appreciate in your life. Guiding ourselves towards the 'glimmers' is a great way to start cementing this. Any gratitude practice asks us to be mindful in the moment, particularly if we aren't present! It also draws our awareness back to the here and now. One way to sustainably cultivate more presence – and over time, depth of presence – is through a daily gratitude practice of your own. This is a beautiful ritual that can be seamlessly sewn into whatever your current schedule contains.

WHAT LESSONS LIE IN HOLDING SPACE FOR OURSELVES?

- Holding space for ourselves teaches us what really matters.
- It teaches us that no matter how hard we think or feel life is, the truth is that it can always get worse.
- It teaches us that life is not linear. I don't know about you, but I'm incredibly grateful for this; it would be pretty uneventful if it was!
- It teaches us the true value of deep presence.
- It teaches us to ground into the invitation *and* gift of being in an in between space, because before we know it, even if it doesn't seem like it will at the time, it will be gone in no time at all.
- It teaches us to notice what pulls us away from being present, as this is where our inner work lies. And, to simultaneously notice what moves us to become more present than ever before, as this is where to fix our focus.
- It teaches us to let go of what is not ours to carry.
- It teaches us that we all have blind spots and these aren't to be ignored. We must take responsibility for our blind spots – recognising that we don't know what we don't know – and hold ourselves accountable for these too. Purposefully acknowledging our privilege, and intentionally integrating our learning in relation to this is lifelong work for us all as human beings, as part of the collective human race.

- It teaches us to be where we are. And, to access an endless source of magic available to all of us in the mundane.
- It teaches us to have reverence for our human experience.
- It teaches us to align with the version of ourselves that we're genuinely feeling called to be, in this lifetime.

'ACTIVE' SURRENDER

I've always found it incredibly ironic that we can covet such heightened aspirations of perfectionism when we are all so, so, *so* different anyway. The fact that we are all different in a myriad of ways is the woven thread that connects us. Ultimately, it is fundamentally our differences that make us the same. However, it is not uncommon for us to wrestle with allowing our own individuality in.

Actively surrendering to what is and what will be allows us to become deeply rooted in our own essence, no matter what is occurring outside of us. We are able to hold duality, nuance, beauty, joy, pain, despair, heartache, hope – all of it – when we are connected to our own humanity, in an unshakeable-kind-of-way. When this is our anchor, it is possible to find a way to dance... not despite it all, but *because* of it. To epitomise what it truly means, to be alive.

A FEW FINAL WORDS

Holding space for ourselves as we navigate the spaces in between is a humbling lesson in being and embracing our whole selves, as humans. That said, I don't profess to be an expert at traversing this bridge! Please take what resonates from what I have shared and leave what doesn't. This chapter is written from my own perspective and lived experience as a white, straight, differently-abled person. I hope it serves you in some way.

ABOUT THE AUTHOR

JESSICA SAVAGE

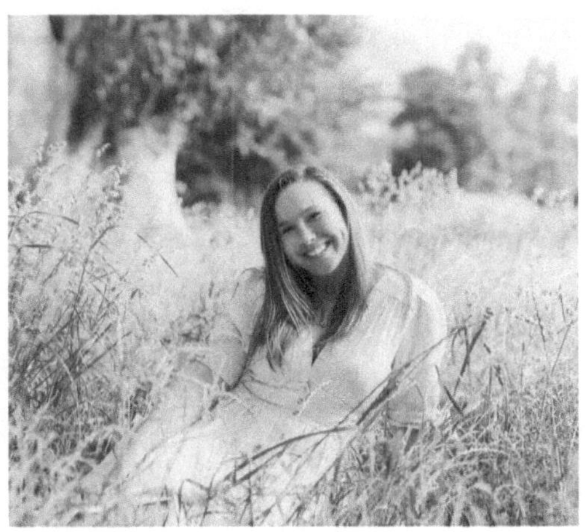

Jessica is a trained life coach and holding space facilitator. She is passionate about social justice and strongly believes in diversity, equity and inclusion learning and integration as a lifelong practice. Her work focuses on being and embracing our whole selves, as humans. In her spare time, Jessica appreciates spending time in nature, reading and revelling in the beauty – and joy of simple, everyday moments shared with her family. Jessica lives with her husband, Cam and their son, Harry in Ōtepoti, Aotearoa New Zealand. She acknowledges Māori as tangata whenua and pays her respects to Ngāi Tahu as the true iwi of the land on which she lives and works from.

jessicalouisesavage

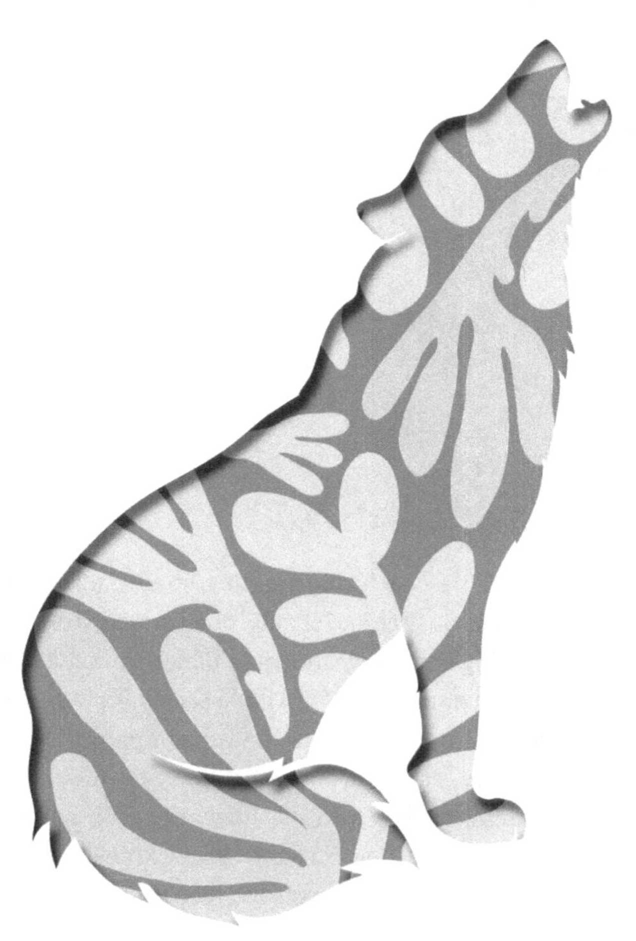

WE ARE MADE UP OF STORIES.

THEY WAIT IN SILENCE TO BE TOLD.

MAY ANTHOLOGIA!

INSPIRE YOU TO TELL YOURS.

www.ingramcontent.com/pod-product-compliance
Lightning Source LLC
Chambersburg PA
CBHW030957210726
48290CB00007B/2351
* 9 7 8 1 7 6 3 5 0 8 3 4 7 *